Zákynthos & Kefaloniá

Front cover: Skála beach, Kefaloniá
Below: Fiskárdo Harbour

TOP 10 ATTRACTIONS

Ássos. This picturesque coastal village sits on a charming natural harbour in Kefaloniá. See page 77.

Zákynthos Museum. Home to many fine icons, frescoes and carvings. See page 28.

Blue Caves, Zákynthos. Swimming here is an unforgettable experience. See page 49.

Vasilikós Peninsula. Beautiful beaches make this part of Zákynthos a popular location for water sports. See page 42.

Mount Énos. Indigenous firs cover the upper reaches of Kefaloniá's highest point. See page 65.

Melissáni. The magnificent cave lake is a highlight of any visit to Kefaloniá. See page 68.

Théatro Avoúri, Zákynthos. Storytelling festivals are held in its three outdoor theatres. See page 38.

West coast road of Kefaloniá. Some of the most spectacular views on the island can be seen from this winding route. See page 74.

Andísamos. This breathtaking bay in Kefaloniá was used as a location for the film *Captain Corelli's Mandolin*. See page 67.

West coast of Zákynthos. A rugged and unspoilt region of traditional hill villages. See page 44.

A PERFECT TOUR of

Day 1   In Town

In the morning visit the Byzantine and Solomos museums and soak up the atmosphere of central Platía Solomoú, before having a light lunch at nearby I Padella. After a siesta, stroll along the seafront for a coffee or cocktail and enjoy a fish dinner at Komis, after viewing dazzling Ágios Dionysos church.

Day 2   Boat tour of the island

Choose from one of the many boat tours that circumnavigate the island, usually in an anti-clockwise direction. This is the best way to admire the stunning coastline of Zákynthos: the two main highlights are the Blue Caves and Shipwreck Bay but look out for the Keri caves too. In the evening, dine at Malanos tavern.

Day 3   Vasilikós Peninsula and Laganás Bay

Rent a car for the rest of the week, starting with a gentle drive down the Vasilikós Peninsula, stopping to visit the Turtle Information Centre at Gérakas and swim at the splendid beach. After lunch at To Triodi, head for another dip at Límni Kerioú, at the far end of Laganás Bay, before some bar action in Laganás.

Day 4   Cape Skinári

Pack your bags and take a drive across the fertile plain to the rugged western mountains, visiting traditional villages, monasteries and the weaving centre at Volímes. Take a dip at the delightful little beach of Xýngi, before driving to the northern tip to Cape Skinári, to stay and eat at the unique Anemomilos converted windmills.

ZAKYNTHOS AND KEFALONIA

Day 5 pm The Southwest

In the afternoon, tour the Palliki Peninsula, swimming at beautiful Petaní beach and taking a late lunch at Xouras. Back in the capital by evening, eat at Kyaní Akti and round the night off at Pub Old House.

Day 6 South coast

Tour along the southern coast, taking an early dip at Trapezáki, visiting the Roman mosaics at Skala and completing the loop via Póros to Sámi. After lunch at a seafront taverna, visit the famous caves of Drogaráti and Melissáni. After a late afternoon dip at the tiny cove of Agía Paraskeví, enjoy a seafood spaghetti at the eponymous taverna or drive back for a meal at To Arhondiko in Argostóli.

Day 7 Wild West

Set off early along the incredibly scenic west coast, so that you can enjoy Mýrtos beach while there is still some shade. Drop into Ássos to admire the harbour and castle, then continue north for a final swim and excellent organic meal at Odisseas in Agía Ierousalím. To avoid driving the twisting coast road at night, it's best to stay at picturesque Fiskárdo.

Day 5 am To Kefaloniá

Put the car on the morning ferry from Ágios Nikólaos to Pesáda on Kefaloniá and settle into your Argostóli hotel.

CONTENTS

INTRODUCTION

The close neighbours of Zákynthos and Kefaloniá do, at first glance, share a great deal: history, geographical proximity and cultural influences. However, to listen to islanders talking you would think they were as different as chalk and cheese. The Zakynthians, according to themselves, are friendly, warm and outgoing, while the Kefalonians are aloof, reserved and suspicious; the Kefalonians, for their part, claim to be proud, independent and hospitable. For all these are stereotypes, imbued with a degree of local rivalry, there is a certain truth to all of the claims.

Even at the level of the landscape, Kefaloniá is more forbidding and mountainous than green, lush Zákynthos. As for the claim that the Zakynthians are more approachable than their neighbours, it is true that the large wave of emigration and subsequent return of richer emigrés has left a much more socially and geographically fractured society on Kefaloniá than on Zákynthos.

Both islands, however, are beautiful and it is likely a visitor will find as much to admire in the wild, rugged west coast of Kefaloniá as in the cosy lowlands of the Central Plain on Zákynthos. Also strong on both islands is a long, vibrant cultural history, seen in their churches, painting and music.

Scented breeze

The oft-quoted Venetian saying 'Zante, Fior di Levante' (Zante, Flower of the East; see page 34) refers to the east wind that carried the perfume of the island's many wild flowers – especially the now-endangered sea daffodils – miles out to sea. The Venetian sailors could therefore smell the island before it came into sight.

Iconic Navágio Bay, Zákynthos

Geology and Environment

Another shared attribute of the islands is their important and unique natural environment. The sea around the islands is beautifully clean, crystal clear and home to two of the most endangered species to be found in Greek waters: the Mediterranean monk seal and the Mediterranean breeding population of the loggerhead turtle (see page 39).

Both islands are predominantly made of heavily folded Cretaceous limestones. Geologically they form a unit, separated from Corfu to the north by the Kefaloniá fault zone. On Zákynthos in particular the island's topography is easily related to the underlying geology. The western mountains are made of relatively hard Cretaceous limestones, while the gentler east is largely made up of Eocene deposits. The Vasilikós Peninsula is a combination of hard Triassic rocks and Plio-Pleistocene marls. Mountainous Kefaloniá largely comprises hard limestones, within which are numerous caves. The heavily folded rocks point to a turbulent geological history, and the islands' location along the Hellenic Subduction Zone gives rise to numerous earthquakes.

As well as being home to several species of mammal (including martens, *Martes foina*, and, on Kefaloniá, feral ponies) the islands

Melissáni cave lake

have a number of interesting reptiles. One of the most spectacular is the large but harmless Aesculapian snake *(Elaphe longissima)*, which can grow up to 2m (6.5ft) in length. Birds include house martins *(Delichon urbica)* and the beautiful golden oriole *(Oriolus oriolus)*. Of the birds of prey, look out for the tiny Scop's owl *(Otus scops)* and the much larger buzzard *(Buteo buteo)*.

The loggerhead turtle

The islands' flora is stunning, especially during spring. Kefaloniá is home to many rare wild flowers, including *Viola cephalonica* and *Campanula garganica-cephalonica*, as well as its own fir, *Abies cephalonica*. Zákynthos is an equally important habitat for flora and still has populations of the fragrant sea daffodil *(Pancratium maritimum)*.

Tourism

On Zákynthos, the first package tourists arrived in 1982, brought by the British company Sunmed and later Club 18–30. This has led to indiscriminate development along the south and east coast beaches of Zákynthos, bringing in its wake a huge annual influx of mostly British package tourists, although numbers have steeply declined in recent years due to the economic crisis. Nonetheless the boom years injected a considerable amount of cash into the local economy, although much of it remains in the hands of the major international tour operators and hotel owners. The tourists also bring unwelcome social behaviour, including bouts of heavy drinking and the occasional fight.

As well as this social disturbance, there has been a huge environmental impact from such a large number of visitors. Prior to the tourist boom the island was extremely poor, with a severely underdeveloped infrastructure. Eager to exploit a steady source of income, locals threw up shoddy hotels and resorts with little regard for their environmental impact, never mind the water and sanitation needs of around 700,000 visitors per year. By the mid-1990s it was realised that action needed to be taken to protect endangered species, such as the loggerhead turtle, and to preserve sensitive areas. After a long, occasionally bitter, campaign by local activists, the Marine National Park of Zákynthos was established in 1999 (see page 40). Over ten years on, there is still friction between ecologists and local businessmen and many of the protective measures that passed in law have not been implemented in practice.

The history of tourism on Kefaloniá is less invasive. It has, so far, largely escaped the ravages of mass package tourism

Mythical Origins

According to Greek mythology, Taphios, the son of Poseidon and Hippothoë, established the city of Taphos on the Peloponnese. Under his son Pterelaus this expanded to include the nearby Ionian islands, and so the inhabitants of Kefaloniá became known as Taphioi. The present-day name is said to come from Cephalus – a son of the king of Ileia – and the names of the four ancient cities (see page 15) from his four sons: Kranius, Paleus, Pronessos and Samos.

As for Zákynthos, Homer reported that Zakynthos was the son of King Dardanos on the Peloponnese. He settled on the island – thus giving it its name – and created the fortification of Psophidia, named after the town in Arcadia from which he came. It is possible that this was on the site of the present-day Bóhali (see page 33).

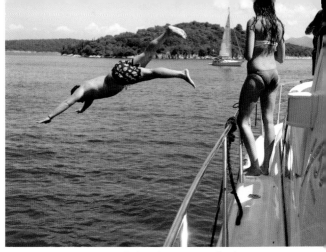
Sailing the exceptionally clear waters

that have afflicted parts of Zákynthos. The relatively low-key tourist developments that do exist are mainly concentrated in Lássi on the west coast, and Skála in the south. The real boost to Kefaloniá's tourism industry came in the mid-1990s with the phenomenal success of the book *Captain Corelli's Mandolin* by Louis de Bernières (see page 70). The descriptions of (pre-war) idyllic island life inspired a large number of visitors to come and see for themselves. Generally fairly affluent, these visitors (mainly from Italy and the UK) have encouraged high-end, and therefore more expensive, development. These tend to be visually kinder to the landscape, though this has resulted in some places, Fiskárdo in particular, becoming overly twee.

Island Life

Though both islands suffer an annual invasion, away from the tourist hordes and outside the peak months of July and August

Taking it easy in Ássos

life carries on much as it does elsewhere in Greece. Many people still farmland for olives and grapes, the harvest for both crops taking place during the autumn and winter.

A number of the local tavernas, at least in the capitals, stay open throughout the winter, and this is the time when islanders tend to go out and enjoy themselves after the hard work of the tourist season. This division of the year does lead to high seasonal unemployment, and some people move to the mainland during the winter. Aside from fishing and agriculture there is little else in terms of industry on either Zákynthos or Kefaloniá – the odd quarry or small-scale food processing – but talk of trying to expand the tourist season, such as offering spring treks to see the islands' flora, has failed to be organised on a practical level.

One traditional aspect of life that still continues is the singing of *kandádes*. These are songs performed by a group of male singers with guitar accompaniment. The music itself is a combination of local traditional songs, Italian popular songs and 19th-century operatic arias (a legacy of Venetian rule). It is not at all unusual to hear Neapolitan favourites such as *O sole mio* in among the Greek offerings. *Arékia*, also popular, is a similar but more thoughtful solo song genre.

A BRIEF HISTORY

Evidence of early human settlement on the southern Ionian islands is scarce. There has been little excavation of specifically palaeolithic and neolithic sites, though a number of artefacts, such as flint hand tools (for example scrapers) have been found, some of which are on display in Argostóli's archaeological museum. The earliest human presence is thought to date from the mid-Palaeolithic era (*c.*50,000 years ago), when, due to ice-age reduction in sea levels, the Ionians were joined to present-day Greece and Italy. It is thought that hunting groups arrived in the region, probably searching for food, from the Píndos (northern Greece) and the Peloponnese. These groups then settled on what are now the islands of Zákynthos and Kefaloniá.

The Bronze Age

Archaeologists now know that there was a thriving Mycenean society on Kefaloniá. As yet, aside from the Bronze-Age tombs close to Kambí on the west coast, there is little corresponding evidence from Zákynthos. It is assumed, backed up by artefacts found during excavations, that the four city-states of ancient Kefaloniá (see box) have their origins in the Late-Helladic period of *c.*1500–1050BC. One of the major centres on Kefaloniá appears to have been near Tzanáta in the southeast, about 8km (5 miles) from the site of Pronnoi, of interest due to its possible links to Odysseus (see box and page 69). Other important sites on Kefaloniá include: the chamber tombs at Mazarakáta, first excavated

Four city-states

Ancient Kefaloniá was a Tetrapolis, comprised of four independent city-states. These were: Pali on present-day Pallíki, Krani near Drápano, Sámi near the port of the same name, and Pronnoi in the south of the island.

The Mycenean tholos tomb near Tzanáta, Kefaloniá

by C.P. de Bosset in 1813; the Late-Helladic chamber tombs at Metaxáta; and the Late-Helladic chamber tomb at Lakíthra, which yielded the richest finds of any of the island's Bronze-Age tombs.

The Archaic, Classical and Hellenic Periods

The origins of the city-states of Kefaloniá and the early rulers of Zákynthos are the subjects of Greek mythology (see page 12). However, there are more recent historical references; Zákynthos and the four city-states of Kefaloniá were mentioned by both Herodotus and Thucydides. Zákynthos seems to have been an independent region, ruled by leaders who originally came from the Peloponnese, possibly nearby Achaia. This independence lasted until just before the outbreak of the Peloponnesian War (431BC), when the island was conquered by the Athenian general Tolmides; it was hence on the side of Athens during most of the conflict.

The pattern on Kefaloniá was more complex. The city-states were generally politically independent of each other and formed their own alliances; Pali alone fought in the Persian Wars, at the battle of Plataea (479BC). However, up until the Peloponnesian War they were all to a greater or lesser extent – but particularly Pali – allied to Corinth. Krani also had links to the Athenians and, on the outbreak of the Peloponnesian War, the whole island was brought under the sphere of Athens.

At some point during the archaic and Classical periods (from c.750BC) the Kefalonian city-states became democratic. Professor G. Moschopoulos notes that the Kefalonian *demos* (citizens eligible to vote – this excluded women and slaves) took part in political decision-making, and that the *vouli* (the city parliament) was the 'dominant institution' in the city of Pali. He also points out that none of the coins from the city-states showed an image of a ruler (except for that of the mythical founder Cephalus; see page 12).

Towards the end of the Peloponnesian War Zákynthos fell under the sphere of Sparta, while the Kefalonian cities wavered in their allegiance between Sparta and Athens, and in 226BC became a member of the Aetolic marine confederation. Later,

Odysseus

The Homeric epic *The Odyssey* follows the adventures of its eponymous hero from Troy, on the coast of Anatolia, back home to mythical Ithaca. For a long time it was assumed that Ithaca was present-day Itháki and numerous local features were named after events in the epic. However, there is no archaeological evidence to back these claims and the latest thinking points to southern Kefaloniá as the most likely spot for the kingdom. Zákynthos is completely out of the running, although it is mentioned by name in both *The Odyssey* and *The Iliad*.

both islands came to the attention of the Macedonians. Philip V occupied Zákynthos – and temporarily lost the island to the Romans during the 2nd Punic War (218–202BC) – but failed to conquer Kefaloniá. The end of Hellenistic influence came when the Romans, under Marcus Fulvius Nobili, conquered Zákynthos in 191BC and Kefaloniá in 189BC.

The Byzantines and Franks

From the point of the Roman invasion to the advent of Byzantine rule in 337AD little of note is recorded in the history of either island. However, the archaeological record shows a certain degree of wealth and artisitic activity, as at the villa at Skála on Kefaloniá (see page 64). Under the Byzantines the islands, Kefaloniá in particular, became active in defending the empire against attack from Arab pirates, and, in 850, Kefaloniá became the head of a *thema*, or administrative district. Zákynthos fared less well during this period, and the sacking of the island by the Vandals in 474 was the first of a number of attacks by outside forces.

As the power of the Byzantines waned, attacks on both islands became more common. In 1085 Robert Guiscard, a Norman leader, attacked Fiskárdo on Kefaloniá, and by 1185 the island was under the rule of the Franks (a disparate group of largely Norman and Italian fiefdoms). In 1204, after the sacking of Constantinople during the infamous Fourth Crusade, Zákynthos followed suit and remained under Frankish rule until 1479. The Frankish rulers of Kefaloniá were a diverse group, at first headed by the Venetian Orsini family, to whom it passed after the Fourth Crusade. In 1357 it was passed, by the King of Naples, to the Tocco family, the most remarkable member of which was Francesca, wife of Carlo I, who reigned after his death, setting up a court of women in Kástro Agíou Georgíou (see page 60).

The Venetian fort at Ássos, Kefaloniá

The Ottomans and Venetians

With the growing power of the Ottoman Turks to the east, it was inevitable that the islands would soon receive their attention, and, in 1479, Zákynthos and Kefaloniá were attacked by Ahmad Pasha. The Ottomans overran the islands, taking many prisoners back to Istanbul. Although the Venetians, then the other major force in the eastern Mediterranean, regained Kefaloniá in 1481, it was ceded back to Sultan Beyazit II in a treaty in 1485.

The Venetians were not deterred from ideas of Mediterranean domination, however, and in 1489 invaded and took over control of Zákynthos. Eleven years later, in 1500, they attacked Kefaloniá with the help of a Spanish army, and, after a two-month siege, took control of Kástro Agíou Georgíou on Christmas Day. Thus, apart from a brief period, the islands are among the few areas of Greece not to have come under Ottoman rule or been noticeably influenced by it.

The two islands remained under the Venetians until 1797. This was a period of relative calm, although the Venetians ensured that both Zákynthos and Kefaloniá were heavily defended; the impressive castles at Bóhali on Zákynthos, and Ássos and Agíou Geórgiou (the long-time Venetian capital) on Kefaloniá are a legacy of Venetian rule. Not only were the islands prized as staging posts for the Venetian navy, they were also useful for their agricultural production and most of the many olive trees now seen on the islands were planted during this time.

One of the most visible legacies of the Venetian occupation is the large number of splendid churches, many with ornate, gilded baroque interiors, found on the islands. Much of the churches' interior decoration and many of their icons, is the work of Cretan sculptors and painters, who fled to Zákynthos and Kefaloniá after Crete fell to the Ottomans in 1669. Once on the two Ionian islands, they came under the influence of the Italian Renaissance and the resulting artistic synthesis is known as Ionian School painting (also known as Heptanese School).

The local rulers came from Venetian aristocratic families, who acquired large estates and settled on the islands. Their names were inscribed in what was called the *Libro d'Oro* (Golden Book). With the greater exposure to the Western world, a number of schools, mostly for religious instruction, were established, bringing the teachings of the enlightenment to the islands. For all this, they were still under autocratic rule and people were not immune from the rumblings of nationalist discontent that grew steadily in the 18th century.

Earthquake zone

'The reason they build their houses so lowe [on Zákynthos] is because of the manifold Earthquakes which doe as much share this Iland as any other place in the World.'
Thomas Coryat, 1612

The Septinsular Republic and the British

This discontent became evident when, in 1797, the islands were occupied by the revolutionary French. The heartening revolutionary fervour with which the islanders greeted the invaders – the *Libro d'Oro* was burnt in Argostóli's main square – initially went into radical proposals such as the abolition of religion. However, the rival powers, specifically the Orthodox Russians, were unhappy about Napoleon's widening sphere of influence and agitation against the French began to ferment. In 1798 a joint Russian and Turkish

Agíou Dionysíou church, Zákynthos Town

fleet sailed for the islands and, with local support, they fell easily to the invaders.

The subsequent Treaty of Constantinople, signed in 1800, ushered in the creation of an autonomous republic under Turkish suzerainty. This, the Eptánisos Politía (or Septinsular Republic), became the first, nominally, independent modern Greek state. Not all went smoothly, however, particularly on Kefaloniá, where Argostóli and Lixoúri were engaged in bitter, sometimes violent, rivalry for political dominance.

The fledgling state came to an end in 1807, when the islands passed back to the French under the Treaty of Tilsit, and in turn Zákynthos and Kefaloniá were

Zákynthos Town in the 19th century, by Joseph Cartwright

occupied by the British in 1809. The British occupation, which lasted until 1863, was not an entirely happy time for the islanders. Although the British did carry out a number of public works (such as building the Ágios Geórgios lighthouse and Drápano bridge near Argostóli), the local population became increasingly unhappy about foreign occupation and rule, especially after the creation of the neighbouring modern Greek state in 1828–32. Although the largely complicit urban middle class had a comfortable standard of living, the peasant farmers were oppressed and poor and, on Kefaloniá in 1848–9, they staged two armed revolts against British rule.

Independence

The two islands had long been a place of refuge for independence fighters from the mainland (the military leader Kolokotronis had landed on Zákynthos in 1805), and in

1863 the islanders' nationalist ambitions were finally realised when the London Protocol declared the Ionian islands part of Greece.

The enlightenment ideals that had spurred the islanders to agitate for independence manifested themselves post-1863 in radical politics. Kefaloniá in particular was a hotbed of dissent and was the home of Marinos Antypas, the 'first Greek socialist', who was murdered in Thessaly in 1907. A more disturbing side of this penchant for radicalism came through in the fascist dictator Ioannnis Metaxas, a native of Kefaloniá, who ruled Greece from a military coup in 1936 until his death in 1941, two months before the German invasion of Greece.

World War II and the 1953 Earthquake

The next 15 years or so were a period of great hardship for the islands, resulting in a large number of families leaving for Australia, the US and South Africa. The first catastrophe was World War II. Although the Greeks initially repulsed and held Mussolini's forces in 1940–41, more powerful joint Axis forces overran the country during 1941. Zákynthos and Kefaloniá were initially under the Italians but when Italy capitulated in 1943 the Germans invaded, imposed a more brutal regime and, on Kefaloniá, executed most of the Italian soldiers (as told in *Captain Corelli's Mandolin*, see page 70).

The islands had just begun to recover from the joint effects of World War II and the ensuing Greek Civil War when, in August 1953, they were struck by a huge

Dionysios Solomos

earthquake. The epicentre was on the seabed between Zákynthos and Kefaloniá, so the impact was felt more in the southern, settled parts of Kefaloniá, and the northern part of Zákynthos, which was relatively unpopulated. The devastation on Kefaloniá was almost total and over 400 people were killed. Zákynthos town was also completely destroyed, not only by the quake itself but also by fire and explosions, due in part to cooking fires and the illegal practice of keeping a box of dynamite under the bed to help with illicit fishing.

Cycling along the Sámi waterfront

The Arrival of Tourism

Many people from the richer island of Kefaloniá emigrated. Far fewer left Zákynthos, which in particular suffered a period of great poverty that only began to lift when, in 1982, the first package tourists arrived. This sparked a wave of indiscriminate tourist development, spreading like a rash along the sandy beaches of the south and east coasts. Kefaloniá was relatively ignored until the phenomenal success of *Captain Corelli's Mandolin* brought tourists to the island in the 1990s, at the same time as emigré Kefalonians began to return from abroad. The environmental dangers of tourism have become more than evident, although ironically it may be the downturn in tourism that saves the day rather than proposed green measures.

Historical Landmarks

c.50,000BC Evidence of palaeolithic settlement.

c.1500–1050BC Establishment of the four city states of Kefaloniá.

191–189BC Conquest of the islands by the Romans.

AD337 The islands come under Byzantine rule.

1185–1479 Frankish occupation of the islands.

1479 Ottomans overrun the islands, taking many locals prisoner.

1489–1500 The Ottomans are driven from the islands (Zákynthos: 1489; Kefaloniá: 1500) by Venetians, never to return. This ensures that the islands are among the few areas of Greece to remain free of Ottoman control and influence.

1500–1797 Era of Venetian rule leads to the appearance of distinctive churches and olive plantations.

1797 The islands are occupied by the revolutionary French.

1798 Russians and Turks, unhappy at Napoleon's widening influence, mount a joint expedition and take the islands from French.

1800 Treaty of Constantinople. The Eptánisos Politía becomes the first autonomous modern Greek state, albeit under Turkish suzerainty.

1807 Treaty of Tilsit. The islands pass back to the French.

1809–63 British occupation of the islands.

1848–9 Two armed revolts against British rule by peasant farmers.

1863 The London Protocol declares the Ionian islands part of Greece.

1941–3 World War II. Greece is occupied initially by Italians, then Germans. Nazi executions of Italian soldiers on Kefaloniá later form inspiration for *Captain Corelli's Mandolin*.

1953 A huge earthquake hits Kefaloniá and Zákynthos, destroying almost all buildings and killing over 400 people.

1982 First package tours arrive on Zákynthos.

1999 National Marine Park of Zákynthos is established.

2000 The movie of *Captain Corelli's Mandolin*, starring Penélope Cruz and Nicholas Cage, is filmed on Kefaloniá.

2012 As the country's economic crisis continues, both islands voted in an anti-bailout far-left MP, a member of the new opposition Syriza party.

ZÁKYNTHOS

Zákynthos, also known by its Italian name Zante, is the southernmost of the Ionian islands that lie off the western coast of mainland Greece. The island divides into three geographical areas: the Vasilikós Peninsula in the southeast, a central plain, and the wild and mountainous north and west. One of the greenest of all the Greek islands, it has good, fertile soil and receives a generous amount of rain in the winter and early spring.

Although Zákynthos is now thoroughly Greek, evidence of the island's Venetian heritage is inescapable, from its Italianate church towers to the descendants of aristocratic Venetian families, still major landowners.

ZÁKYNTHOS TOWN

The once-elegant harbour town of **Zákynthos ❶** had its public buildings and squares rebuilt approximately as they were before the 1953 earthquake, but in reinforced concrete. Ferries from Kyllíni pull in at the long jetty at the southern end of the harbour, where the port authority can also be found.

Running parallel to the harbour is the main shopping street of Alex. Románou where you will find most of the upmarket boutiques and jewellers. Románou ends at Platía Agíou Márkou, which adjoins Platía Solomoú.

The Byzantine Museum of Zákynthos

Platía Solomoú is the focus of the northern end of the harbourfront, around which the town's museums and municipal buildings are clustered. On Platía Solomoú is

View of Zákynthos port and town

the **Byzantine Museum of Zákynthos** Ⓐ (Tue–Sun 8am–2.30pm; charge), also known simply as the Zákynthos Museum. It contains many pieces from the old Pandokrátora Museum, as well as frescoes, icons and carvings rescued from churches devastated in the 1953 earthquake. There are also 17th- to 19th-century religious paintings of the Ionian School, founded by Cretan artists fleeing the Ottoman conquest who met local artists strongly influenced by the Italian Renaissance.

Start in the room on your right as you go in. Here you will find a wonderful carved iconostasis by Angelos Mosketis (1683). This was rescued from the church of Pandokrátora (1517), and alongside are photos of the damage to the church caused by the earthquake, and of its reconstruction. The other impressive iconostasis at the end of the room dates from 1690 and is from Agíou Dimítrios tou Kóla (both churches are in Zákynthos Town). There is also a splendid icon of the Virgin from the same church.

As you climb the stairs to the first floor there is a room off to the left, full of icons. A number of these, on the right, came from the old museum. There are some very fine Venetian-inspired paintings from Agías Ekaterínis tou Grypári in Zákynthos Town, and 16th-century icons from Agíou Pnévmatos in Gaïtáni. Perhaps the most interesting work here is the 17th-century representation of Jerusalem from Agías Ekaterínis ton Kípon, Zákynthos Town. Look closely and you will see that this is a very Christian representation of the holy city, with no evidence of its Muslim heritage to be seen.

Two-faced island

While Zákynthos's beautiful sandy beaches, concentrated on its southern and eastern coasts, are popular with package holidaymakers, the rest of the island – especially the west coast – remains rugged and, for the most part, undeveloped.

Zákynthos town harbourfront

On the first floor you begin in a small room which contains carved Byzantine stonework (10th- to 11th-century), one piece of which shows the Byzantine double-headed eagle. Then you enter what is possibly the museum's star exhibit, the fabulous, fully frescoed interior of the monastery church of Agíou Andréa in Mesovoúni Volimón. The church itself is 16th century, while the paintings date from the 17th century. The frescoed interior is set out as it was in situ and a number of precious sacred vessels are laid out in front of the apse.

There follows a long corridor with a display of silver censers. The first bay contains rescued frescoes from Agíou Georgíou ton Kalogrión (1669); there are also two panels, one of St Nicholas and one of two angels with a scroll, from Agías Ánnas (1715). The second bay has a superb series of icons rescued from across the island. Particularly notable are the Panagía i Amólyndos from Agíou Nikólaou tou Mólou, the

17th-century Ágios Ioánnis o Hrysóstomos from Agíou Ioánni tou Tráfou, and the 17th-century Ascension of the Virgin from the old museum.

The next bay holds late 17th- to 18th-century icons, including a splendid 18th-century one of Jonah and the Whale from Agíou Spyrídona tou Flabouriári. The final bay is given over to 12 baroque paintings from the iconostasis of Agíon Anargýron by Nikolaos Koutouzis (1741–1813) and Nikolaos Kantounis (1767–1834). On the way down the stairs, on the left, are Kantounis' paintings from Agíou Georgíou ton Kalogrión.

The final room, on the ground floor, houses a notable

A 17th-century Ionian School icon in the Zákynthos Museum

model of Zákynthos Town before the 1953 earthquake, giving a good idea of its attractive Italianate character before it was destroyed. On the walls are paintings by Koutzouzis from the church of Agíou Spyrídona tou Flabouriári.

The Library

Next to the town's theatre, also on Platía Solomoú, is the **Library** (Mon–Wed 12pm–7pm, Thur–Sat 8.30am–1pm), where there is a small display of photographs showing the island pre-1953. As well as views of the town and the lavish interiors of some of the island's churches, there are photos of the elegant interiors of the mansions of the Zakynthian Italian aristocracy, in particular those of the now destroyed town palace of the locally prominent Komoutou family. At the top of the stairs is a small room with a rather bizarre collection of dolls in what purports

Home to rest

In 1960 the bodies of Andreas Kalvos and his English wife were brought to Zákynthos from Keddington, in Lincolnshire, where the poet had spent much of his life.

to be traditional Zakynthian dress (strictly speaking there is no such thing).

Close to the Library, on the corner of the square by the sea, is the reconstructed church of **Agíou Nikólaou tou Mólou**. The attractive stone building is worth a quick visit. However, many of its original icons are now housed in the nearby Byzantine Museum of Zakynthos.

The Solomos Museum

Set back from Platía Solomoú is Platía Agíou Márkou, with a number of cafés, on the far side of which is the **Museum of Dionysios Solomos and Andreas Kalvos** ❸ (daily 9am–2pm; charge). Named after Greece's national poet, the museum is dedicated to famous Zakynthians – these are noticeably male, and in most cases, famous in local terms only. Inside, on the left, are the rather grand tombs of Solomos and Andreas Kalvos, a fellow poet (see box).

The main body of the museum lies upstairs. The room in front of you is dedicated to the fine icon collection of Nikolaos and Thaleia Kolyvos. On the right is a room containing set and costume designs for productions of the work of the playwright Dionysios Romas. The gallery given over to exhibits on Solomos himself (writer of the lyrics of the Greek national anthem and a champion of Demotic Greek) has a number of portraits, samples of his handwriting and, more bizarrely, a glass urn containing earth from his first grave in

Corfu. Visitors might be surprised to notice that many of the manuscripts are in Italian, his first language. It was only with his rising nationalist consciousness that he turned to writing in Greek.

Further on, there is an interesting case containing memorabilia of the operetta composer and musician Pavlos Karreri (1829–96), otherwise known as Paul Carrer. Close by, there is an imposing coloured lithograph of *The Great Battle of 'Garibaldin' at Siatista under the Leadership of Alexandros Romas'*, next to which is a portrait of Romas himself, looking disturbingly like Joseph Stalin.

Moní Agíou Dionysíou

On the seafront, at the southern end of the harbour, is the most important church of Zákynthos town, **Agíou Dionysíou** Ⓒ (daily 8am–1pm, 5–10pm; free). It was founded by monks living in seclusion on one of the islands of Strofádes (80km/50 miles south of Zákynthos), where they had been guarding the body of the Zakynthian Ágios Dionýsios. In 1717, to escape the attacks of pirates, they brought the body to Zákynthos and re-established their monastery. In 1764 the church was remodelled, and a bell tower built beside it in 1854. However, the church was completely destroyed in an earthquake in 1893. The present church – an earthquake-proof building – was completed in 1948 and was one of the very few buildings to survive the 1953 earthquake.

The church's interior, although modern, is well worth a look. Every inch is covered with paintings and gilding. Around the church, over the tops of the pillars, are a series of panels describing the exploits of the saint, as well as of the relic of his body. One of the more bizarre episodes shows the monks using the desiccated body of the saint to expel a plague of locusts. On the right-hand side of the nave is a small chapel containing the grave of the saint. The impressive silver coffin was made in 1829 by Diamantis Bafas. He also made the silver surrounds for the icons on the church's intricately carved wooden iconostasis. The saint has two festival days, celebrated on 24 August and 17 December.

Bóhali Froúrio

Above the town in the Bóhali district, is the huge Venetian **Froúrio ⓓ**, or fort (daily 8am–2.30pm; charge). Thought to stand on the site of ancient Psophida, the fortress has Byzantine antecedents, but any traces of these earlier settlements – with the exception of the 12th-century church of the Pandokrátor – have been destroyed by earthquakes. The present fortifications were built under the Venetian *Proveditor general da mar* Giovanni Battisto Grimani and finished in 1646. As a prime defensive site, the fort served as a place of refuge

The Froúrio walls

for local people and, particularly in the 17th century, became a flourishing settlement. The fort fell into disuse in 1864, when Zákynthos became part of the Greek Republic.

The Froúrio lies at the end of a winding road that leads up from the town through Bóhali village. Just before the top of the hill is the village *platía* in front of the church, with a few cafés and tavernas that have a lovely view over Zákynthos Town and harbour. The inside of the fort is now a beautiful pine wood, and you have to search around for the remains of the buildings (there is a useful site plan at the entrance). However, perhaps the main reason for coming up to the Froúrio is the spectacular panoramic view. The site's slow renovation by the EU and Greek Ministry of Culture has ground to a halt and shorter opening hours mean sunsets

Sonnet – To Zante

Fair isle, that from the fairest of all flowers,
Thy gentlest of all gentle names dost take!
How many memories of what radiant hours
At sight of thee and thine at once awake!
How many scenes of what departed bliss!
How many thoughts of what entombéd hopes!
How many visions of a maiden that is
No more – no more upon thy verdant slopes!
No more! Alas, that magical sad sound
Transforming all! Thy charms shall please no more –
Thy memory no more! Acccurséd ground
Henceforth I hold thy flower-enamelled shore,
O hyacinthine isle! O purple Zante!
'Isola d'oro! Fior di Levante!'

Edgar Allan Poe, 1837

must be enjoyed from the cafés below.

On the way up Bóhali hill, on the left-hand side coming from town, is the **Zákynthos Nautical Museum** (daily 9am–2pm, 6–9pm; charge). The work of one man, the museum tells the history of Greek seafaring through a series of model boats, as well as an eclectic assortment of naval artefacts.

Vines are intensively cultivated in these parts

CENTRAL PLAIN

The island's central plain is the most fertile in the Ionian Islands. It is mostly given over to the intensive cultivation of vines and, away from the resorts and airport, is sprinkled with attractive little villages. Separating the plain from the eastern coast is a line of steep but low hills, and on the western side the mountains rise sharply and dramatically. Along the foot of mountains lie a string of villages, many located at points where springs emerge from the hills above.

The central villages include sleepy little Gaïtáni with an attractive Italianate church, and a characteristic separate bell tower, which dates from 1906. Similar architecture can be seen in neighbouring tiny settlements of Vanáto and Hourhoulídi. The detached bell towers seen across the island are built away from the church to prevent the bells falling through its roof in the event of an earthquake.

On the road between Zákynthos Town and Maherádo is the **Ktíma Agría Komoútou** (daily 9am–1pm, 5pm–8pm; free). There has been a vineyard belonging to the Komoútou family

Caper *(káppari)* buds and flowers

on this spot since 1638 but it was the present owner's father who established the commercial winery, which now produces some of the best wines on the island. You can watch the production of the wines, as well as taste and buy them. Much of the cultivation is organic and there is also good olive oil for sale.

Maherádo, Agía Marína and Pigadákia

At the foot of the steep climb up to Kiliómeno is the large village of **Maherádo**, home to a couple of interesting churches and some surviving, albeit decaying, examples of traditional pre-earthquake architecture. The village square by the church of Agías Mávras has two nearby cafés serving basic food such as *souvláki*, salad and *tzatzíki*.

The main sight in Maherádo was the pilgrimage church of **Agías Mávras**. The icon of Agía Mávra was supposedly found on this spot and a church built around it. However, a devastating fire in 2005 destroyed the roof and much of the baroque interior by Nikolaos Latsis. Some of the contents were saved and it is still in the process of being restored. The festival of Agía Mávra, who is said to help healing, is celebrated at the beginning of June.

On the left-hand side, just after turning up the hill towards Kiliómeno, is a modern convent whose church has an attractively painted interior. Wrap-around skirts are provided for visitors whose dress is not modest enough for a church visit.

North of Maherádo, and higher up the mountainside, is the village of **Agía Marína**. The eponymous church has an impressive interior but is often locked. Also here is the **Hélmi Museum of Natural History** (May–Oct daily 9am–6pm, Nov–Apr 9am–2pm; charge), with a small but informative display on the flora and fauna of the island.

Further on is **Pigadákia** ❷, named after its springs (*pigí* in Greek). The lovely 16th-century church of **Agíou Pandelímona** has a holy spring in the saint's shrine under the altar, said to promote healing; this is one of the few places where you can go behind the iconostasis. The traditional *papadosiakoús* dance is performed at the saint's festival on 27 July. The **Vertzagio Museum** (Mar–Nov daily 9am–2pm, Sun–Fri 6–8pm; charge) here has a motley display of rural artefacts.

Gerakári, Kypséli and Tragáki

Three pretty hilltop villages sit on the slopes in the north of the plain. They are **Gerakári**, **Kypséli** and **Tragáki**, the southernmost, largest and most strung out. They all give splendid views over the plain below. One of the few places to eat, with basic food, is Harry's *kafenío* and *psistaría* in Tragáki.

Just north of tiny Limodaíka (near Tragáki) is the **Théatro Avoúri/Skaliá Cultural Centre** ❸ (tel: 26950 62973). Established by local actor and storyteller Dimitris Avouris in 1995, the beautiful site has three

View from Gerakári church

stone-built outdoor theatres, which hold from 60 to 1,000 people, as well as a new indoor auditorium. There are storytelling performances four times a week and, as well as holding Greek and pan-European storytelling festivals, the theatre played its part in the 2004 Cultural Olympiad by hosting global storytelling events.

The East Coast

Leaving Zákynthos Town heading north, you pass through **Kryonéri**, along the seafront. The water is reasonably clean, especially given its proximity to the harbour, and the locals swim off the rocks and narrow pebbly beach here. After the steep climb up to pleasant, strung-out Akrotíri, the road runs inland along the ridge before descending back down to the sea at **Tsiliví**. This is the first of a string of resorts and not the most pleasant. Situated on a lovely bay with a decent beach, Tsiliví is dominated by loud bars, shops peddling tourist souvenirs and holidaymakers going red in the sun. Tsiliví blends seamlessly into Plános before things quieten down a bit at Boúka.

After the small promontory of Akrotírio Gáidaros, for the next 4km (2.5 miles) between Aboúla and Amoúdi, the road passes turn-offs to a string of small, quiet beaches. There are rooms to rent at most of them, and there are a couple of excellent beachside tavernas. About 1km (0.6 miles) beyond Amoúdi is **Alikaná**, perhaps the most pleasant of the resorts along this coast. Towards the sea it is still fairly quiet and the mountain backdrop is lovely.

At the northernmost point of the Central Plain is the large resort of **Alykés**. A larger version of Tsiliví, Alykés has all the facilities expected of a Greek package resort – cheap accommodation, all-day English breakfasts and football on satellite TV. It is, however, on a sweeping bay with a sandy beach and views of Kefaloniá. The exposed bay attracts windsurfers and can produce some surf. This is also one of places you can take a boat to the Blue Caves near Skinári (trips are advertised everywhere; see page 49). Behind the town are the old salt-works, the large pans forming shallow lakes where salt was obtained from seawater through evaporation. These are now no longer used, as it is cheaper to import salt from the mainland. Consequently, the stagnant water can be rather smelly.

LAGANÁS BAY

If you dislike mass tourism and loud nightclubs, the place you will most want to avoid on Zákynthos is **Laganás**. Ironically, this, the island's most notorious resort, is right in the middle of its most environmentally sensitive area. It is estimated that Zákynthos receives up to 700,000 visitors every year, half of whom stay in Laganás on the south coast. They come for the wonderful sandy beach that stretches from the Vasilikós

Laganás is known for its nightlife

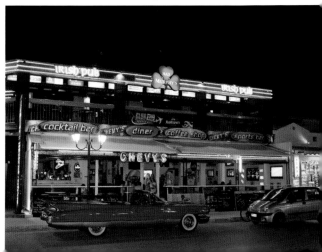

Peninsula in the east to Límni Kerioú beach in the west. This lively nightspot – or den of iniquity, depending on your point of view – is brash, noisy and nocturnal. Apart from its crowded beach, the resort's main attraction is its nightlife; one of the more popular spots is on the island of Ágios Sóstis, joined to the shore by a walkway. **Kalamáki**, 4km (2.5 miles) east of Laganás, is perhaps the most pleasant of the hectic resorts on this side of the bay.

National Marine Park

In response to these conflicting demands on the bay – and after intense campaigning by local environmentalists – in

National Park Rules

Within the confines of the National Park, you must not:
• fish
• light a fire
• camp
• pick any plants
• throw away ANY rubbish

On turtle nesting beaches there is:
• no access between sunset and sunrise
• no use of umbrellas 5m (16ft) from the waterline
• no digging in the sand
• no disturbing the cages protecting the nests
• no use of any vehicle
• no access to horses
• no access to dogs without a leash
• no use of ANY lights at night

Access and speed is restricted for boats across the whole area. The strictly protected area around Sekánia has access only for scientists with permission.

1999 the Greek government established the **National Marine Park of Zákynthos** ❹, the country's first. The protected area takes in: the marine area and beaches of Laganás Bay, and around capes Marathiá and Yérakas at either end; an area of land stretching back from the beach, and behind that a buffer zone that extends almost as far as Zákynthos

The National Park logo

Town; and the Strofádes Islands 80km (50 miles) to the south. The park's effectiveness has periodically been compromised due to frequent funding shortages that often leave it unstaffed and unprotected. Thankfully the crusading Gérakas Turtle Information Centre (see page 43) monitors the situation.

However, the entire bay is the most important nesting site for the loggerhead turtle *(Caretta caretta)* in the Mediterranean basin. The turtles are very sensitive to human disturbance and have suffered greatly from the indiscriminate development of this coast.

The turtles roam throughout the Mediterranean (there is evidence to suggest they use the Gulf of Gabés off Tunisia as a wintering ground) and in the spring return to Laganás Bay to nest. They rest and mate in the bay while waiting to come ashore during the night. After nightfall, the females crawl up the beach to find a suitable nesting site in the soft sand; if they are disturbed by noises or lights they will return to the sea without laying any eggs. If they are not disturbed, they dig a deep hole and lay a clutch of about 120 eggs. These take about two months to hatch, after which the hatchlings dig their way to surface and – at night – make their way down to the sea.

Conflicts with humans arise not only due to pressures of space, forcing the turtles on to fewer beaches and raising the nesting density, but particularly due to disturbance of the nests themselves and, once the turtles have emerged from their shells, from light pollution. The hatchlings find their way to the sea using reflected starlight on the water. Any shoreside lighting confuses the tiny turtles, causing them to make their way inland, where they die.

The park is home not only to the famous turtles but also the critically endangered Mediterranean monk seal (11–12 of which inhabit sea caves outside of the park), and is important as a rest stop for migrating birds. It also protects certain species of plants, particularly the sea daffodil (*Pancratium maritimum*) and the seabed cover of Posidonia (*Posidonia oceania*), which contributes a large part of the oxygen in the Mediterranean. The habitat of **Lake Kerí** (Límni Kerioú) is the last remaining wetland of Zákynthos, important for migrating bird species. There used to be a huge lake behind Laganás that stretched almost as far as Zákynthos Town, but this was drained in an act of environmental vandalism to make way for the airport.

The Vasilikós Peninsula

On the eastern side of Laganás Bay is one of the most beautiful parts of the island, the **Vasilikós Peninsula**. Heading south from Zákynthos Town the first place you come to is the resort of Argási, which has suffered more than most places from the tourism decline. As the land starts to rise, things begin to improve. Set against the backdrop of Mount Skopós, there are a string of beautiful small beaches along the northern edge of the peninsula. The longest of these, Paralía Iónio, is near the strung-out village of Vasilikós. Iónio runs into the nudist Banana Beach, and around the cape from here is the popular water sports centre at **Ágios Nikoláos**. On the opposite side of the bay is the unsympathetic development at Pórto Róma.

The best beach, however, is on the southwestern side at **Gérakas** ❺, a superb sweep of sand fringed by cliffs. There is only one problem – this corner of paradise is an important nesting site for turtles. Access is controlled by a park ranger en route to the beach, and numbers are limited to protect the nests. For those who want to get even closer to nature, the far end of the beach is nudist.

The exemplary **Gérakas Turtle Information Centre**, run by the environmental organisation Earth, Sea and Sky, provides information on the turtles and the other flora and fauna of the peninsula. They can also advise on

Gérakas beach, where turtle nests are protected

joining volunteer environmental protection programmes (see page 88).

Further back up the peninsula's west coast is the isolated beach of Dáfni, with a pleasant *psarotavérna*, reached by a very rough road from Vasilikós. Between Dáfni and Kalamaki is the totally protected beach of Sekánia (access is only given to scientists with prior permission).

THE HILL VILLAGES AND WEST COAST

The wild and mountainous west coast is the least-spoilt part of the island, with hillsides covered in bright green *maquis*

The cliffs at Cape Kerí

and small, dry-stone-walled fields. The land falls to the sea in precipitous cliffs, with no easily accessible beaches; one reason why it has so far resisted tourist development. The sea caves at the foot of the cliffs are used for breeding by the very few remaining pairs of Mediterranean monk seals (*Monarchus monarchus*). This, and the so-far near-pristine environment, are the reasons why environmentalists are lobbying for protected status (like that for Laganás Bay) for this region.

The hill villages retain much of their traditional architecture and character. Many pre-earthquake buildings survive, though most are too dangerous to live in. One factor that has contributed to their preservation is that no-one can use the damaged buildings unless they have the permission of the owners.

Kerí and Agalás

On the western side of the southern cape – best crossed by the spectacular but rough road from Marathiá – is the pretty village of **Kerí** ❻. Many of the traditional houses here have been bought up by German and British visitors, giving the village quite a different, and more reserved, character from other places on the island. As well as a 17th-century church, Kerí is known for the *píssa tou Keríou*, or natural tar pools, mentioned by both Herodotus and Pliny. Now dried up, they were previously used for caulking boats. A couple of kilometres down the road is the lighthouse at Cape Kerí.

The minor road north from the village runs through a very attractive wooded valley. It leads to the quiet village of **Agalás**, tucked away in the southwestern part of the island. Next to the church in the centre is the small maritime and natural history museum and art gallery, though, with its erratic opening times you may have to ask around for the key. Further south into the village, at the point where the KTEL buses drop off and pick up, you'll find a café and taverna. Signposted off from the village are some Venetian wells and the Damiános cave; both down towards the sea.

Kilioméno and Loúha

At the top of the long, steep climb from Maherádo (see page 36) is **Kilioméno** ❼. On the right-hand side, just before the road turns for Ágios Léon, is Korfiatos, a wooden balcony with lovely views, where you can have a drink or simple meal. Behind the benches, which seem more Bavarian than Greek, are huge barrels of local wine. As well as the wine there is also excellent local olive oil and thyme honey for sale. Opposite is Kilioméno's rather odd-looking church of Ágios Nikólaos, with its still-unfinished bell tower.

Venetian ruins

One notable feature of the landscape is the ruined stone towers on the tops of the hills. These are the remains of Venetian windmills, previously used for pumping water up from wells.

Loúha village

Leaving Kilioméno, the road turns sharp right and leads to the friendly, if a little lacklustre, village of Ágios Léon. Look out for the Venetian windmill converted into a church tower. A road heading inland from here goes up to **Loúha ❽**, one of the highest, and certainly one of the prettiest, settlements on Zákynthos. The domestic architecture of the hill villages differs from that of the rest of the island; plain exteriors hide pretty courtyards, usually full of flowers, with the living quarters set around them. To get a better look at this arrangement pay a visit to Loúha's tiny village shop and post office (opposite the church of Ioánnis Theológos). The courtyard behind, with a 400-year-old floor, has an attractive taverna on the first floor (with the added bonus of excellent toilets). The previously equally attractive village of Gýrio, just beyond Loúha, has been rather spoilt by a breeze-block factory.

The majority of Zákynthos's high mountain villages are controlled by the KKE (Greek communist party). The communists have organised collective agricultural cooperatives to help local farmers buy machinery, and then harvest and market their produce

From Ágios Léon a pretty but winding, and initially very narrow, road leads down to **Limniónas** by the sea. All that is here is a taverna that looks out over a beautiful rocky bay. Beside the taverna a flight of steps leads down to a small bathing platform.

Éxo Hóra to Anafonítria

The main road carries on north to **Éxo Hóra**. At the crossroads at the village centre is a huge olive tree, reputedly the oldest on the island. The crossroads is also the turn-off for **Kambí**, where a large concrete cross glowers down on the sea from a tall headland. The cross commemorates the place where right-wing soldiers threw a group of local communists to their death in the war, or vice versa, depending whose version of the story you believe.

The unspoilt village of **Mariés** lies further north. Local legend claims Mary Magdalena landed here on her way to or from Rome. This accounts for what seems to be a disproportionate number of churches for the village's size, and for its name (derived from María).

Where the road turns east towards the village of Orthoniés, there is a turn left for **Anafonítria ❾**. Ágios Dionýsios was abbot at the 14th-century monastery here from 1578 to his death in 1622. Further on, above the turn for Navágio, is the 16th-century monastery of **Ágios Geórgios ton Krimnón**, with its striking round tower.

Navágio Bay

Just beyond Anafonítria is the headland overlooking **Navágio Bay** (Shipwreck Bay) ❿, on which is the most photographed beach in the Ionians – a sheltered bay where a rusty freighter lies half-buried in sand. The locals take great exception to the disfigurement of their spectacular beach (it was previously known as Paradise Beach) and decry the fact that the boat is now regarded as a tourist icon – it was scuttled by an unscrupulous captain, allegedly a smuggler, for a fraudulent insurance claim.

However, looking down the sheer cliffs from the small steel-viewing platform above is quite spectacular and, for anyone with even a mild distrust of heights, quite stomach churning. Boat trips shuttle sightseers to the beach from **Pórto Vrómi**, below Mariés. The bigger operators are perhaps best avoided for environmental reasons; boats above a certain size are not supposed to land on the beach, but they invariably do.

Back on the main road, heading further north brings you to Volímes (see page 49).

THE NORTH

North of Alykés the landscape becomes more desolate, rugged and deserted. It was this part of the island that felt the

The Blue Caves

strongest tremors of the 1953 earthquake; the epicentre was in the channel between northern Zákynthos and Kefaloniá.

Odorous beach

The sulphurous smell that wafts around the coast at the tiny bay of Xýngi – surrounded by steep walls of rock – emanates from a hot spring in one of the nearby sea caves.

The long climb out of **Katastári** (the largest village outside the capital) gives views back to Alykés Bay and over to Kefaloniá. After passing the 16th-century Moní Ágios Ioánnis Prodrómou, with an important icon by Theodore Poulakis, you reach the turn-off for Mariés. The road that heads over to the west coast passes through some stunning scenery.

The road along the east coast then plunges down a very steep (10 percent) hill, passing by **Xýngi** ⓫ (see box) and around a headland with numerous sea caves, to the beach at **Makrýs Gialós**. Here, there is a camping ground, several places to eat and sea caves you can swim into right by the beach. About 0.5km (550 yards) further on is the tiny headland of **Kokkínou**, where you can pick up a *kaïki* (boat) to the Blue Caves and eat overlooking the boats bobbing in the small inlet. Beyond Kokkínou is the turn-off for the two mountain villages of **Volímes**, famous for their honey and textiles, as well as their surviving traditional mountain architecture.

The road hugs the coast from here to the small port of **Ágios Nikólaos**, where there are summer ferries to Kefaloniá, but it is best to get boats to the **Blue Caves** ⓬ from the spectacularly located lighthouse at Cape Skinári, the extreme northern tip of the island. The water in the caves appears bright blue, and appears to colour your skin as you swim (see also page 39).

KEFALONIÁ

Dramatic, rugged and mountainous, Kefaloniá is the largest and highest Ionian island, rising to 1,627m (5,338ft) at the summit of Mount Énos. Although, or perhaps because, tourism is a relatively recent phenomenon on the island, sparked off in part by the book and film, *Captain Corelli's Mandolin* (see page 70), Kefaloniá has one of the least spoilt environments and some of the best beaches in the Ionian Islands. The south is dominated by the heights of Mount Énos, bordered on the west by the Livathó Plain. In the west is the quiet Pallíki Peninsula, while the stunning north coast is fringed by dramatic cliffs.

ARGOSTÓLI

The island's capital, and also its largest town, **Argostóli** ❶ was completely destroyed in the 1953 earthquake and has been rebuilt largely with modern concrete buildings. Although it is essentially a port and administrative centre, the town is not entirely devoid of charm. It has a great position on the Argostóli Gulf surrounded by mountains, has a number of interesting museums, and makes a good base for exploring the rest of the island. Life in Argostóli centres around Platia Valiánou (the central square) and the

Seismic emigration

The 1953 earthquake devastated almost all of Kefaloniá – except the far north – causing a huge exodus of refugees. Many settled in Australia, Canada and the US, although recent years have seen families returning to the island.

The Ávythos lake, between Póros and Sámi

Ancient trade link

One of the most interesting exhibits in Room 2 of the Archaeological Museum is an Egyptian scarab from the reign of Tuthmosis III (1504–1450BC). It was found in a Mycenaean site at Kráni, indicating that there was trade between Kefaloniá and pharonic Egypt.

pedestrianised shopping street of Lithóstroto.

The Archaeological Museum

On P. Vergóti, close to the theatre and opposite the beginning of Lithóstroto, is Argostóli's **Archaeological Museum Ⓐ** (Tue–Sun 8.30am–3pm; charge). Although small – the museum has just three rooms – the finds are well displayed and help to build up a picture of Kefaloniá's ancient history.

The first room has artefacts from the Palaeolithic to Mycenaean periods and on the left-hand wall are some interesting archive photos (1899–1933) of excavations on the island. The pieces on display range from very early flint hand tools (100,000–40,000 years old), to clay figurines (c.3rd century BC) from the cult centre of the Nymphs at the Drákinas Cave near Póros. The cave had been a settlement from late Neolithic times (8,000BC onwards). The final case has finds (mostly *kantharos*, or double-handled pots) from the late-middle Helladic cist (box-shaped) graves (1750–1700BC) and Mycenaean tholos (beehive) tombs at Kokkoláta, southeast of Argostóli.

Room 2 is given over to finds from Mycenaean, or Mycenaean-influenced sites. By now the visitor will have noticed a certain grave and tomb theme to the exhibits. Perhaps the most important finds in this room come from the tholos tomb at Tzannáta near Póros. These include some delicately beaten gold, one piece of which shows the Mycenaean double-axe, clay figurines and an intriguing bronze buckle, indicating the existence of a powerful Mycenaean centre, probably related to Homeric Ithaca. It is thought that this will be vital evidence in pinpointing the exact location of the mythical kingdom.

The third and final room has displays of pieces from the Classical and Roman eras. On the left are a few larger exhibits, including a charming trident and dolphin floor mosaic from the 2nd-century BC sanctuary of Poseidon at Váltsa, on the Pallíki Peninsula. The cases on the right mostly contain pieces from the four ancient cities of Kefaloniá (see page 15). Notable exhibits include an exquisite gold, winged Niké from Menegáta, a marble head of Silenus from Skiniás and a Roman 3rd-century AD bronze male head from Sámi.

The Korgialénios Museum

Up the hill, past the theatre, is the fascinating **Korgialénios Museum and Library** ⓑ (Ilía Zervoú; Mon–Sat 9am–2pm;

A 19th-century view of Argostóli by Joseph Cartwright

charge). Set up after the 1953 earthquake to house objects salvaged from the wreckage, the museum gives an overview of 19th-century Kefalonian domestic life. One of the refreshing aspects of the museum is its concentration on the lives and world of Kefalonian women, albeit mostly of the urban middle class. To this end, the displays start with a case of household linen, as well as items such as kid gloves, silk stockings and hairpins. What follows is an amazing collection of urban women's costume between 1878 and 1910. They are displayed in period interiors, which give an excellent impression of the life of the Kefalonian aristocracy at the end of the 19th century.

Strolling down Lithóstroto, Argostóli

For the most part, the dresses are highly elaborate and beautifully made in lace, silk and satin, with appliqué. There is a lovely pair of bridal shoes from 1905 and particularly exquisite is a young girl's ball gown of 1894, with silk tulle and embroidered roses. There are also a great number of accessories, including shawls, fans, parasols and gloves.

The museum also has a good display of photographs of pre-1953 Argostóli. The earliest, from 1904–6 and taken by local photographer N. Trikardos, show it as a neat, provincial town. Some of the later (1930s) pictures were taken by two members of the Kosmetatou family. More disturbing are the images showing the total devastation of the town after the 1953 earthquake.

Other displays include a room with some rather dark and heavy furniture and portraits of local worthies, a lovely 18th-century carved

No-nonsense praise

'The buildings of Argostóli are handsome, and the town, though not remarkable for its liveliness, possesses many good streets and public edifices.'
Edward Lear, *Views in the Seven Ionian Islands*, 1863

and painted wooden iconostasis from the church of Agíou Georgíou, and a case with the effects of Dimitrios Korgialenios (died 1861), a member of the secret pro-independence Filikí Etería (Society of Friends). Finally, after a cluttered but cosy reconstruction of a traditional bedroom, there are displays of agricultural implements.

The Foká-Kosmetátou Foundation

Back towards the central *platía*, at the far end of Valliánou, is a beautifully restored neoclassical mansion housing the **Foká-Kosmetátou Foundation** C (May–Oct Mon–Sat 9.30am–1pm; charge). The foundation, which was established in 1984 from the estates of three brothers, turned their family home into a museum to display their private collections and to publish studies on Kefaloniá; it has also established the Votanókypos Kefaloniás on the outskirts of town (see page 59).

The museum consists of just one room with, on the right, a display of Greek numismatics and, opposite, a number of lithographs of the Ionians and some pieces of furniture that belonged to the family. Of greatest interest are the lithographs by Joseph Cartwright, Edward Lear and Henry Cook, all of whom published volumes of paintings and engravings of the Ionians. Close by is a fine icon of Ágios Vikédios attributed to Theodoros Poulakis. Also look out for the 10 drachma bank

Drápono Bridge

note from the 1890s, cut in half; each half then became worth five drachmas. The small but pretty garden at the back is used to hold temporary exhibitions.

Lithóstroto and the Drápano Bridge

The main shopping street of Argostóli is the pedestrianised **Lithóstroto**, which runs south from P. Vergóti, the site of the town's theatre. Reconstructed after the 1953 earthquake, during the 19th and early-20th century the theatre, with its largely Italian opera productions, was the centre of the social life of Argostóli's middle class. Lithóstroto is lined with cafés, rivals to those in the central *platía*, and pricey clothing and shoe shops. About halfway down, on the right-hand side, is the town's Catholic church. Heavily restored following the earth-quake, its chief claim to fame is the 14th-century icon of the Panagía Prevezána. Beyond the church is the **Pýrgos Kabánas** (Kabána Tower). This reconstructed late 18th-century Venetian bell tower now houses a pleasant café decorated with pre-earthquake photographs of Argostóli. The café was created by the municipality and is run as part of the ROTA Cooperative, which places people with mental illness in jobs in the community. On offer are a few local specialities, such as *soumáda* and the Kefalonian *amygdalópita* (almond pie).

At the end of the pedestrianised section of Lithóstroto, turn left down towards the harbour. On the left is the town's produce market. Depending on the season it is piled high with all kinds of colourful agricultural produce.

Walking south along the water brings you to the **Drápano Bridge**. This stone-built causeway crosses the shallow Koútavos Lagoon but is closed due to structural damage. Built by the British in 1810, it was overseen by Major de Bosset, Commandant of Kefaloniá, a Swiss soldier in the service of the British army. The obelisk in the centre has an inscription to the supposed glories of the British Empire.

The *Katavóthres*

Rizospáston heads north from the central *platía*. On your right you will pass Argostóli's **Filarmonikí Skholí** (Philharmonic School), and opposite, on the corner of the next block, the only building to have survived the 1953 earthquake intact. The streets running off to the right will take you down to the harbour.

By the port authority buildings (near where the ferries depart) is Argostóli's helpful **EOT** (tourist information office). Further along, past the place on the quay where you catch the ferry for Lixoúri, is a line of *estiatória* (restaurants), the best of

Column of light

On a short promontory at Cape Ágios Theódoros is a Doric-colonnaded lighthouse dating from 1820. It was commissioned by Charles Napier, who was the British Governor of Kefaloniá between 1822 and 1830.

The *katavóthres* (sea mills) near Argostóli

which is Kyani Akti (see page 108). Before that, on the left, is a small square. On a small patch of grass is the marble base of a Venetian fountain, with carved lions' heads. The column above it is of later (19th-century) provenance.

Continue along the coast, past a couple of very pleasant tavernas and down a pine-shaded footpath beside the rocks, where local people swim in the evening. After about a kilometre (0.6 miles), you reach the tip of the cape. The views here over the mountains and the Argostóli Gulf are spectacular. Also here are the **katavóthres ❷**, or sea mills, which are the product of a bizarre geological phenomenon. Seawater from the gulf disappears down a series of small sinkholes, only to re-emerge in the cave of Melissáni and under the Gulf of Sámi on the opposite side of the island. The water passes through channels cut by subterranean fresh-water streams during the last ice age, when seawater levels were lower. Fresh water filtering down through the limestone hills increases the flow. As the channels widen the now-brackish water slows, before its resurgence.

The current at the Argostóli end was strong enough in the past to drive mills, built by the British to grind grain. After the 1953 earthquake the flow was disrupted and slowed to the gently running channels you see today. The original mills were destroyed in 1953 and replaced by a fake water wheel and a café, very popular with locals for Sunday lunch. Further on, around the cape, are a series of small bays where you can swim.

Votanókypos Kefaloniás

Leaving town to the south, following Leofóros Georgíou Vergóti, brings you to a fork in the road. The left carries on to Peratáta, the right-hand turn has a signpost to the **Votanókypos Kefaloniás ❸** (Cephalonia Botanica; Tue–Sat 10am–2pm, 6pm–8pm; charge). Follow the signs and don't be put off by the rough track, as it soon levels out. Bear left at the top of the rise and the site is 50m (160ft) along on your right. Entrance is free with a ticket to the Foká-Kosmetátou Foundation (see page 55), otherwise leave your money in the honesty box in the hut at the entrance.

This botanical garden was established in 2000 in an old olive grove. Its aim is to represent the rich flora of the different environments found on Kefaloniá, as well as seeking to preserve rare and endangered Kefalonian plants. The garden is allied to the Millennium Seed Bank at London's Kew Gardens. The site

The gardens at Votanókypos Kefaloniás

is beautiful and a world away from the nearby warehouses on the main road. An artificial stream runs through the centre of well laid-out and labelled areas, while in spring and early summer it is lovely to see the floor of the remaining olive grove carpeted with flowers, rather than the ploughed-up versions usually seen from the roadside.

THE LIVATHÓ AND SOUTH COAST

To the south of Argostóli is the **Livathó Plain**, one of the few level areas on the island. Not surprisingly it is largely given over to agriculture. The road out of town bisects the plain, passing the castle of Agíou Georgíou above the villages of Peratáta and Mazarakáta (site of a Mycenaean necropolis), before, dominated by the bulk of Mount Énos to the east, it hugs the southern coast along to the resort of Skála.

Kástro Agíou Georgíou

Towering above the plain is the **Kástro Agíou Georgíou ❹** (mid-June–Oct Tue–Sun 8am–2.30pm; charge), constantly being renovated and liable to closure. The fortress stands on

Kástro Agíou Georgíou

a pine-clad hill, and can be reached from the north by the turn-off for the Robola Wine Cooperative or via the hairpinned road from Peratáta. Either route brings you up to the Bórgo, the village outside the castle's walls. The view from the top is spectacular, and either the Castle or Memories café/bar is a good place to take it in, particularly if you have just walked up in the heat and are in need of refreshment.

There has been a fortress on the site since Byzantine times, centred around the church of Agíou Georgíou from which the castle takes its name. In 1185 the island was taken by the Franks, and the fort was controlled by them until 1485. After a brief period of Turkish rule, the castle passed to the Venetians in 1500 following a three-month siege. The fortifications seen today largely date from the period of Venetian occupation. At this time the castle was the centre of the island's administration, but in 1757 the Venetians moved

Icon from Moní Agíou Andréou

their official headquarters down to Argostóli, heralding the fort's decline. Like all buildings in southern Kefaloniá, the castle suffered great damage in the 1953 earthquake. However, it is well worth a visit for the view and renovated walls.

Back down in Peratáta, just beyond the village, is the turn for **Moní Agíou Andréou** (also confusingly known as **Moní Milapidiás**). The convent is now housed in modern (post-1953) buildings. Opposite these is the old church of Ágios Andréas, home to important 16th- to 18th-century icons by, among others, Immanuel Lambardos and Athanassios Anninos (1713–48). These are now part of the **Ecclesiatical Museum** (daily 9am–1.30pm, 5pm–8pm; charge). As well as good Ionian School paintings, the well-laid-out museum has

The beach at Lássi

reliquaries allegedly containing remains of Ágios Andréas and some ecclesiastical vestments.

Lássi and Metaxáta

A low but steep range of hills separates the Livathó Plain and Argostóli from the west coast. This hides some pretty villages, a couple of good wineries and, on the western side, attractive beaches. From Argostóli take either the main road out towards Lakíthra (then follow the signposts to the airport), or go around the cape via Ágios Theódoros and a number of bays, along a pleasant pine-flanked road. Both routes are walkable and will bring you to Lássi, the closest resort to Argostóli.

By Greek island standards **Lássi** is fairly low-key, although it does get crowded in high season. The star beaches here are **Makrýs** and **Platýs Gialós**, both with fine sand and clean, blue water. The latter has a small island attached to the beach by a short isthmus. The coastal road continues south above cliffs with lovely views. After a couple of kilometres (1.2 miles) is the **Gentilini Winery** (tours and tastings May, June and mid-Sept–Oct, Tue, Thur and Sat 5.30–8.30pm; July–mid-Sept Mon–Sat 10am–2.30pm and 5.30–8.30pm). Owned by the Kosmetatou family, the winery was established in 1984 and specialises in high-quality organic wines, including a fine Robola.

Above Miniá, close to the airport, is the pretty village of Sarláta, topped by a rather Gothic, ivy-clad ruin. There are a number of rooms and villas to let here. Just along from Sarláta is **Domáta**, with an impressive church and houses spilling down the hillside. The church of the Panagía here contains the coffin in which the remains of Patriarch Grigoris V were transported from Istanbul to Odessa. It also has an interesting 19th-century wooden iconostasis.

The next village is **Metaxáta**, chiefly famous as the place where Byron stayed for four months in 1823 before leaving for Mesolóngi on the mainland, where he died. A bust of the poet can be seen in the main square, close to the site of the house where he stayed (destroyed in 1953). Below Metaxáta and Domáta is **Kourkoumeláta**, close to the lovely beach of Ávythos. The attractive village was rebuilt by Andreas Vergotis after 1953. At **Pesáda**, where seasonal ferries leave for Ágios Nikólaos on Zákynthos, is the **Divino Winery** (summer daily 10am–8pm) which produces a traditional Muscat, made from sun-dried grapes.

Lourdáta to Skála

From the long beach at **Lourdáta**, just past Pesáda, to the village of Markópoulo there is little apart from **Moní Theotókou Sisíon**, believed to have been founded by St Francis of Assisi. The road south from here is fairly bleak, though towards the coast the land appears more fertile. After the right turn-off to Skála, the road rises towards **Markópoulo ❺**. The church of the Panagía here is the scene of a bizarre festival. Between the

Pebbled shoreline between Póros and Skála

6th and 15th of August hundreds of small, harmless snakes appear, said to bring good luck to the village.

Taking the left-hand turn to Skála takes you first past **Kateliós**, and then the long sweep of sand of **Kamínia**. Before reaching Kateliós you might want to call in at the **Metaxas Wine Estate** (May–Oct daily 10.30am–6pm) and taste their excellent Robola. Kateliós is a tiny, laid-back resort with a lovely sandy beach, on the opposite side of the bay from Kamínia. This is Kefaloniá's most important nesting beach for loggerhead turtles, although fewer nest here than on Zákynthos. Visitors should treat this area with respect and follow the national park guidelines (see page 40). In truth it shouldn't be necessary to disturb the turtles as just along the coast is **Skála**, a popular, but relatively tasteful resort on a huge sandy beach backed by pine-clad hills. Also here, a little inland, are the excavated remains of a Roman villa with some fine, preserved mosaics.

MOUNT ÉNOS

The highest mountain in the Ionian islands is **Mount Énos ⑥**. At 1,627m (5,338ft) it dominates the southern part of Kefaloniá. Also known by its Venetian name of Monte Nero (the black mountain), its upper reaches are covered by the Greek fir *(Abies cephalonica)*, giving the mountain a dark cap. The fir was first identified on the island (hence its Latin name) and the Énos population is particularly important due to its lack of hybridisation. It is generally found at altitudes of between 800 and 1,600m (2,600–5,250ft) and grows up to 30m (100ft) high. It was an important tree to the ancient Greeks, who used it extensively in shipbuilding.

Énos National Park

The indigenous population of firs is now protected by the **Énos National Park**. This takes in the summit of Mount Énos above 1,000m (3,280ft) and the northern flanks of neighbouring Mount Roúdi (also called Gioúpari; 1,124m/3,687ft). The two mountains are divided by a high saddle, which is marred by a NATO radar station bristling with satellite dishes. A new tarmac road runs up to the saddle from the main road between Argostóli and Sámi. From the telecom masts it's another 1km (0.6 miles) downhill on an unpaved road to a car park, from where a signposted footpath ascends to the summit, named Megas Soros. If it is not too hazy

Goats on the flanks of Mount Énos

Feral ponies

The semi-wild ponies of Mount Énos are descended from animals abandoned after World War II. They initially formed communities of up to 100 animals but are now highly endangered, numbering only some 12–14 individuals. If you are lucky enough to spot them, be careful not to disturb them.

the views from the top are incomparable.

The turn-off towards Valsamáta will take you to the **Cephalonian Robola Producers Cooperative ❼** at Frangáta (summer daily 7am–8.30pm, winter daily 7am–3pm). The Robola grape is cultivated on the high altitude limestone soils found in the region and is used to produce a fine white wine. The cooperative makes two Robola wines, both of which can be tasted in the visitors' centre.

Close to the winery, just beyond Valsamáta, is **Moní Agíou Gerasímou**. Ágios Gerasímos is the patron saint of Kefaloniá, and the convent, founded in the 16th century, is the most important pilgrimage site on the island. The (male) saint founded a female order in 1554 and was beatified in 1622.

Inside the new convent church, consecrated in 1992, is the saint's silver shrine, inside which is the reliquary containing his bones; his funeral robes are draped over the shrine. Although the church is new, it still contains many fine original works of art, as well as a staircase that descends to a couple of small chambers, thought to be the saint's sanctuary.

SÁMI AND PÓROS

The road from Argostóli over the flanks of Mount Énos descends past fir-clad slopes to the small port of **Sámi**. Ferries leave from here for the island of Itháki and Pátra, on the mainland. Sámi is a pleasant, quiet town with a few eating places along the harbourfront. This town was the location for much of the filming of *Captain Corelli's Mandolin* in 2000 (see page

70). For the filming, much of Sámi's pre-earthquake architecture was reconstructed, only to be destroyed during the subsequent battle scenes.

Over the headland of Cape Dihália (also known as Mýtikas) is the beautiful white shingle beach of **Andísamos** ❽, also used as a location for the film. Surrounded by steep, *maquis*-clad hills, the deep inlet looks out on the southern coast of Itháki. The clear water is great for swimming; the furthest little bay of the beach is nudist.

The Drogaráti and Melissáni Caves

On the road from Argostóli, about 3km (2 miles) before Sámi, is the turn for the **Drogaráti Cave** ❾ (Apr–Oct daily 9am–5pm; charge). The cave was discovered about 300 years ago, after an earthquake opened up the present entrance. A steep series of steps leads down into a cool fissure, at the bottom of

Melissáni cave lake

which is a concrete viewing platform overlooking the huge chamber. Occasionally used to hold concerts, it has an impressive array of stalactites. Some of these are damaged, broken off by unthinking souvenir hunters, but there is still a huge amount of flowstone left. From the platform you can make your way down on to the floor of the chamber, where you can explore the nooks and crannies. To see the chamber at its best, wait until the tour groups have departed, when you can explore on your own.

Perhaps even more impressive is the cave lake at **Melissáni** ❿ (May–Oct daily 9am–5pm, Nov–Apr Fri–Sun 10am–4pm; charge), north of Sámi. A short artificial tunnel brings you to the edge of a large underground lake, partly open to the sky due to the collapse of the cavern's roof; the sunlight on the deep, clear water turns it an iridescent blue. Visitors are rowed around the lake by waiting boatmen.

The cave was formed between 20,000 and 16,000 years ago, during the last ice age. The roof of the cavern collapsed some 5,000 years ago, the debris from which still lies in the centre of the lake. Perhaps the most fascinating aspect of its geology is that it is the point of resurgence for the water that sinks at the katavóthres near Argostóli, hence the water in the cave is brackish. It enters the lake at its deepest point (32m/104ft) on the left-hand side, and sinks again at the far point of the covered section of the cave which lies to your right.

It was in the still intact section of the cavern that archaeological finds were made, dating from the 4th–3rd century BC, confirming that the cave had been the site of a cult of Pan and the Nymphs. These are now in Argostóli Archaeological Museum (see page 52).

From the cave, near Karavómylos, the coast road runs north around the bay of Sámi, to the small port of **Agía Efimía Ierous**. This attractive yachting harbour has a great location, with steep, bare mountainsides looming behind and a sweeping view over the bay to Itháki. The town's narrow shingle beach, north of the yachting harbour – now backed by rather brutal concrete sea walls – has wonderfully clear water and the swimming here is excellent.

Póros

The main road south from Sámi passes through some beautiful countryside, as well as the attractive mountain villages of Digaléto and Ágios Nikólaos, which are close to the **Ávythos Lake**. Just beyond Ágios Nikólaos, on the hairpin bends, are the ruins of a monastery. From here the road runs straight down to the village of Tzanáta.

At Agía Efimía

Tzanáta lies in a fertile bowl. On a small rise in the vale is a Mycenaean tholos (beehive) tomb, excavated in 1992–4. The earliest finds date from c.1350BC and the high quality of the artefacts – including jewellery, pottery and seals – points to the existence of a powerful Mycenaean centre. It is thought that this may identify Tzanáta as the location of Homeric Ithaca.

Between Tzanáta and Póros the road passes through the short but impressive 80-m (260-ft) deep **Póros Gorge ⓫**, the channel for a seasonal river. The town of **Póros** is divided by a rocky headland, on the far side of which is the port and fishing harbour. Ferries sail from here to Kyllíni on the mainland.

The Remetzo café/bar at the foot of the jetty is pleasant and also has surprisingly good toilets. As a resort, Póros has a quiet, pleasantly run-down air. The 2-km (1.2-mile) long pebbly town beach has very clear water and there are some secluded rocky bays around the headland.

To the north of town is the long beach of Rágia, above which is **Moní Theotókou Átrou** (take the right turn just after the gorge on leaving town). This is said to be the oldest

Captain Corelli's Mandolin

This novel, by the British author Louis de Bernières and set in Kefaloniá during World War II, was first published in 1994 and became a bestseller through word of mouth. The book concerns the exploits of Antonio Corelli, a mandolin-playing captain in the occupying Italian army, and Pelagia, daughter of the local doctor. The core of the text is a love story but this is also set against the German invasion of 1943, after the capitulation of the Italians, and the subsequent massacre of Italian troops, and any islander found helping them, by the German army. Add in the Greek communist resistance, a ridiculous upper-class English intelligence officer who can only speak ancient Greek and a film tie-in starring Nicolas Cage and Penélope Cruz, shot on location on Kefaloniá, and you have the Captain Corelli phenomenon.

Although the book has been an international success with the reading public (despite being famously slow to get into), it has stirred up the passions of locals and historians alike. Their major objection is the book's portrayal of the communist resistance (known by the acronym ELAS). Well-loved and regarded as national heroes by many Greeks – and aided in this case by Italian fighters – its portrayal in the book is suspect. The strong anti-communist – and historically inaccurate – bias to the text slanders not only the movement as a whole, but, more specifically, a surviving partisan, Amos Pampaloni, on whose life it seems to have been based, and who objected strongly to this historical mistreatment.

monastery on Kefaloniá, first mentioned in 1264. The beautiful road south to Skála runs along the deserted coastline. Before reaching Skála, at Ágios Geórgios, there are the (minimal) remains of a classical temple to Apollo.

THE PALLÍKI PENINSULA

Soaking up the rays on Póros beach

On the opposite (western) side of the gulf from Argostóli is the large Pallíki Peninsula, which, away from its south coast, is barely touched by tourism. On the southeast coast is its major town, Argostóli's traditional rival Lixoúri.

Lixoúri

Easily reached by an hourly ferry (around 20 minutes), **Lixoúri** now plays second fiddle to Argostóli and is a sleepy, laid-back place. However, it's worth taking the ferry for the views of the gulf alone and there are a number of sights worth seeing in the town. It is also a good jumping off point for other places on the peninsula.

Lixoúri developed under Venetian rule (becoming officially recognised in 1534), but about 1.5km (1 mile) north of town is the site of ancient Pali, one of the four ancient city states of the island (see page 15). Much of Lixoúri was destroyed in 1953 but a few major buildings have been reconstructed as before. The earliest of these is the collonaded Markáto, just behind the seafront where the Argostóli ferry docks. It was built in 1824 by the British governor, Charles Napier, and was Kefaloniá's first courtroom.

Xí beach

Further along, on Grígoris Labráki, is the **Filarmonikí Skholí Pállis** (Philharmonic School), in a fine neoclassical building dated 1836 (rebuilt in 1963). There are four such 'schools' – wind and brass ensembles, a legacy of British rule – on the island: here, in Argostóli, and in Sámi and Póros. Wind instruments including the flute of founder, Petros Skarlatos (1820–1904), are on show in the prettily decorated first-floor rehearsal room.

Also in the town, up the hill on Ekaterínis (from the port walk up Pávlou Dellapórta, then Mihaïl Avílhou) is the **Lixoúri Museum and Library** (Tue–Sat 9.30am–1pm; charge). Set in an attractive 1866 neoclassical building with a shady garden, the library holds around 25,000 volumes. The attached museum has three early gospels, as well as 18th- and 19th-century ecclesiastical vestments.

On the waterfront is a statue of local satirical writer and poet Andreas Laskaratos (1811–1901), his back turned on

Argostóli across the water. The early nationalist writer Elias Miniates (1669–1714) was also born here.

The South and East Coasts

To the south is the plain of Katogís, the most fertile area on the island, planted with wheat and vines. This suffered greatly in the 1953 earthquake and the effect on the now-fractured topography is obvious. The southern coast has some lovely beaches, and the most popular and spectacular are the red sand stretches of **Mégas Lákkos** and its continuation, **Xí ⑫**.

North of Xí is the village of Madzavináta, unremarkable except for the **Vitoratos Winery** (summer daily 10am–2pm and 6–8pm). Beyond Madzaninata is **Havriáta**. As well as the church of **Iperagías Theotókou**, it is the location of the school of Vikentiou Damodou (1700–52), one of the first on the island. Back towards Lixoúri is **Soullári**, with its church of Agías Marínas, dating from 1600 and containing icons by the Cretan painters Immanuel Moskos and Theodoros Poulakis. The water dripping down in the cave at Moní Agías Paraskevís, by the beach at **Lépeda**, allegedly cures eye infections.

North of town, past the port of ancient Pali at Karavostási, is the monastery of the Panagías at **Kehriónos**; a festival is held here on 23 August. Opposite is the **Sclavos Winery** (daily in summer, 7pm–9pm). Some 5km (3 miles) further on is a small but important wetland area near the village of **Livádi**.

Anogí

The northern and western mountainous part of the peninsula is known as Anogí. At the southern end of the

No more rocking

Just along from Xí beach, close to Cape Akrotíri, is the Kounópetra (the name literally means, 'rocking stone'). This flat slab of stone used to rock in the waves, but the 1953 earthquake disturbed its balance, so that it no longer moves.

wild and deserted west coast is the monastery of **Theotókou Kipouríon**, founded in 1759. Perched high on the cliffs, this can be a spectacular place to watch the sunset. Below is the sea cave of **Drakospiliá** (dragon's cave). There is a spring at the nearby ruined church of Agía Paraskeví that is said to cure stomach ailments. Some 10km (6 miles) up the coast – longer by the winding roads – is undoubtedly the finest beach on the peninsula, **Petaní** ⓭, a beautiful stretch of pebbles backed by steep cliffs.

Before reaching Petaní you pass through the village of **Kodogenáda**. In addition to its restored 18th- and 19th-century vernacular architecture, the village is home to two important churches, the 12th- to 13th-century Agíou Georgíou and Agíou Ioánni tou Theológou, with its impressive carved iconostasis.

THE NORTH

The north of Kefaloniá escaped the worst of the ravages of the 1953 earthquake and so has much surviving traditional architecture. The landscape is barren and spectacularly steep, particularly along the **west coast road**, which is the best, if most alarming, ride on the island.

Northwest Coast Villages

From Argostóli the road takes you past the turning for the village of **Davgáta**, the location of the **Museum of Natural History** (summer Mon–Fri 9am–1.30pm,, Sat–Sun 9am–1pm; winter Sun–Fri 9am–1.30pm; charge). Set up as an educational centre and library, it provides a useful introduction to the local geology, flora and fauna.

The coast road continues to Fársa, where it starts to climb. Above is the old village, ruined in 1953. Below, and along this whole stretch of coast, you can see rows of fish farms. Beyond

The bay of Mýrtos

Angónas the view along the northwest coast opens up – a steep line of cliffs falling into blue sea. Down to the west are the beaches of **Agía Kyriakí** and **Voúti**. The long, exposed stretch of sand at Agía Kyriakí can attract flotsam but the small bay at Voúti, down a rough unmade road from the village of Zóla, is cleaner. Although the water isn't the island's clearest, it can get very warm here, even in early summer.

From here onward the sharp hairpins of the road hug the cliff edges. This is Kefaloniá's equivalent of the oceanside Highway 1 in California. The views – back to the largely inaccessible north coast of Pallíki and forward to Ássos – are wonderful.

Mýrtos and Ássos

Some 10km (6 miles) beyond Angónas the road turns sharply inland, forming a large hairpin around the truly spectacular bay of **Mýrtos ⑭**. The best place to see the beach and cliffs is from the lay-by on the main road on the northern side of the bay. Looking down, you see a crescent of bright white beach bordered by the cornflower blue of the sea and surrounded by sheer cliffs. The way down to the beach is via the steep but well-paved road from Divaráta. Once there, it does not quite live up to its view from above. What appeared to be white sand turns out to be small pebbles, and it can get very busy. The beach also feels too organised, with sunbeds, a café and lifeguards – essential, as the sea can be dangerous here.

From Divaráta the road continues east (turn left before the village to go north). The road crosses the island, through a gap in the mountains, to Agía Efimía (see page 68), passing on the way a couple of now derelict Venetian windmills that were previously used for pumping water up from wells.

The road north carries on in a similarly spectacular fashion. About 3km (2 miles) after a viewpoint lay-bay is the steep descent to **Ássos** 🅑. At the bottom is Ássos village, with its

View of Ássos

charming natural harbour. The village retains much of its traditional architecture (reconstructed with the help of the City of Paris, commemorated by a plaque in Platía Parísion), and in spring and early summer is covered in flowers. The small beach

Picturesque prison

Dating from the late 16th century, the fortress at Ássos was used as a prison until 1953. The prisoners tended the vines that covered the hillsides and clifftops above Ássos village.

in the harbour is fairly clean but just round the coast are some beautiful coves, only accessible by boat.

Connected to the village by a short isthmus is an enormous Venetian *kástro* (fort) on top of a hill. Begun in 1593, it served to protect the Venetian fleet and island from attack by the Ottomans and pirates. In more recent history it was used as a prison (see box). The winding path takes you up through pine woods and gives fine views over the harbour and neighbouring coast. Apart from the walls and the lovely curving entrance, little remains inside the fort, although a new visitors' centre has been sensitively built in the middle.

Around Fiskárdo

The road beyond Ássos ends up at the harbour of Fiskárdo at the northeastern tip of the island. This is perhaps the most immediately attractive part of the island, with much surviving traditional vernacular architecture. Two of the most attractive **hill villages** here are **Vasilikiádes**, on the main road 10km (6 miles) before Fiskárdo, and **Mesovoúnia**. The latter is on the eastern road to Agía Efimía. This passes through a string of very pretty mountain villages – **Varý**, **Karyá** and **Komitáta** – and the views over to the neighbouring island of Itháki are magnificent. The only sounds across this landscape, with its dry stone walls and abandoned stone houses, are the tinkling of cow and sheep bells. Water is at a premium here, and there

Fiskárdo harbour

are a number of rainwater cisterns with concrete covered catchments above. The view down to Agía Efimía from Komitáta is breathtaking.

Towards Fiskárdo itself you pass through **Mánganos**, with its excellent greengrocer (O Manganaras), full of wonderful local fruit and vegetables, and olives, oil and wine, and **Andipáta Erísou**, location of a superb estiatorío, To Pefko (see page 111), and the turn-off for Dafnoúdi beach (see page 79). **Fiskárdo** ⓰ itself survived the 1953 earthquake intact, and has cashed in on this with a vengeance. The admittedly very attractive harbourfront is backed by pastel-shaded housing, now largely expensive restaurants, cafés and boutiques. The harbour, for better or worse, is also greatly beloved by yachters, particularly those on flotilla holidays (it's fun to sit on the quayside watching novice sailors try to bring their boats in for mooring).

The port takes its name from Robert Guiscard, a Norman soldier who died here in 1085, but is thought to be the location of ancient Panormas. There is also a Roman cemetery (2nd–4th centuries AD). Towards the Venetian lighthouse, on the northern headland, is an interesting church, started by the Byzantines, but largely Norman in execution (c.12th century). At the southern end of the harbour is the **Nautical and Environmental Museum** (summer Mon–Fri 10am–6pm, Sun 10am–2pm; donations encouraged). Run by volunteers from the FNEC European exchange programme, it consists of one room with some interesting exhibits, including the skeleton of a Cuvier's beaked whale, found dead on Émblisi beach in 1995, and displays describing local birds and mammals and their habitats.

The northern coast has some wonderful small and quiet **beaches**, all of which have the clearest imaginable water. Some of the little bays, with their white pebble beaches, are only accessible by boat (easily hired for the day in Fiskárdo from Regina's boats). The two most easily accessible from Fiskárdo are, to the north, **Émblisi** and, to the south, the beautiful bay of **Fóki**. Heavenly **Dafnoúdi** is reached by a 20-minute walk down through pine trees from the village of Andipáta Erísou. Tiny **Alatiés**, to the south of Dafnoúdi, could be lovely, but attracts tar (and an unfortunate smell), but nearby **Agía Ierousalím** ⑰ is a lot cleaner and has one of the friendliest tavernas on the island, Odisseas (see page 110).

Fiskárdo waterfront by night

ITHÁKI

Easily visited from Kefaloniá, the island of Itháki has a history that's intimately tied up with that of its larger neighbour. Claimed by many, particularly the locals, to be the mythical homeland of the Homeric hero Odysseus, there is little archaeological evidence to support this claim (indeed, it seems as though Homeric Ithaca is likely to lie close to present-day Póros on Kefaloniá, see page 69). Daily ferries leave from Sámi on Kefaloniá and dock at the tiny harbour of Píso Aetós on the west coast of Itháki.

Like Kefaloniá, Itháki suffered greatly from the 1953 earthquake, causing many people to emigrate (the population dropped from around 15,000 to under 3,000). However, it is a supremely beautiful and unspoilt island with a lovely main town, Vathý, and some gorgeous deserted beaches.

Vathý and the North

Vathý ⓱ lies on the island's east coast, at the head of a deep bay on the Gulf of Mólou. It is a quiet, very attractive town (it still retains surviving pre-earthquake architecture) with a huge number of tavernas set around its harbourfront and an **Archaeological Museum** (Tue–Sun 8.30am–3pm; free). Ferries depart for Pátra on the mainland.

To the north, the road crosses the isthmus and either heads up to the mountain-top village of Anogí or around the western coast through Léfki.

Twin peaks

Itháki is essentially two groups of mountains linked by a narrow isthmus. On the eastern side of the isthmus is the deep Gulf of Mólou, while on the north coast is the large bay of Afáles.

Vathý harbour

Anogí, only occupied for half the year, has fabulous views as well as the Byzantine church of Kímisis tis Theotókou. Before reaching Léfki you pass a series of small, quiet pebble beaches: Vrýsi, Áspros Gialós, Komninoú Ámmos and Koutoúpi.

The roads from both Léfki and Anogí join at **Stavrós**, the island's second-largest town. This sits above the small port of Pólis (a 20-minute walk). There is a small **Archaeological Museum** (Tue–Sun 8.30am–3pm; free) here, housing local finds. These mostly come from the early Bronze Age to Mycenaean site at nearby Pelikáta, one of the many sites claimed as the location of the palace of Odysseus.

North of Stavrós a road winds up to the hill village of Exogí. On the way up is an excavation known as the School of Homer, in reality a tower dating from the 6th century BC; close by is a Mycenaean tomb. Below is the spectacular bay of **Afáles** with its lovely beach. From the beach at Afáles a rough, but beautiful minor road heads north towards Cape Drákou Pídimia, before doubling back down to the deserted beach at Mármaka.

After the quiet port of Fríkes on the east coast, a favourite yachting harbour, the main road heads around to **Kióni** ❷⓿, an attractive place and Itháki's most upmarket resort. Like Fiskárdo on Kefaloniá, Kióni survived the 1953 earthquake, and has capitalised on this in a similar fashion, as evidenced in the prices for accommodation. The coast between Fríkes and Kióni has a number of lovely pebbly beaches. The walk up to Anogí from Kióni, along a clearly marked path, is delightful and takes around 1.5 hours each way.

Itháki's main town, Vathý

The Odysseus Trail

The south of the island has a number of sites that are supposedly linked with events in Homer's *The Odyssey* (see page 17). Close to Vathý, up the hill from the beach at Dexá (identified as ancient Phorcys, the landing place of Odysseus), is the **Cave of the Nymphs** ㉑. This spot is apparently where the Greek hero, helped by the goddess Athene, hid the cauldrons, tripods, cloaks and cups given to him by the Phaeacian king, Alcinous.

Odysseus, transformed by the goddess into an old man, met up with Eumaeus (his old palace swineherd) at the

Venetian windmills near Kióni

Arethoúsa Spring ㉒, where the pigs were being watered. The spring is in the south of the island, 3km (2 miles) from Vathý, along a steep but well-marked path. Above the spring is the Cave of Eumaeus.

On the other side of the island, towards the harbour and pebble beach at **Píso Aetós**, is the site of **Alalkomenes** (*c.*700BC). This was wrongly identified by the German archaeologist Heinrich Schliemann in 1878 as the palace of Odysseus, where the hero came to win back his wife, Penelope, from her suitors.

Above Píso Aetós is the village of **Perahóri**, which is close to the island's now deserted and ruined medieval capital, Paleóhora.

WHAT TO DO

SPORTS

The wonderfully clear sea and spectacular mountains of Zákynthos and Kefaloniá invite visitors to do more than just sit in a deck chair looking out at the view. Options for active holidays are numerous, from swimming, diving and sailing to walking, cycling and horse riding.

Water sports

Swimming. The water quality around the islands is excellent. The water is extremely clear and clean and, in general, safe; though be careful at some of the west-facing beaches, particularly Mýrtos on Kefaloniá, as there can be some very nasty undercurrents. For little children, the southern and eastern beaches of Zákynthos (for example Kalamáki, Pórto Koúkla and Tsiliví) are best, as they have gently sloping sand and calm waters. Otherwise, most hotels and many apartments have swimming pools, though in summer it would be a shame not to take advantage of the warm waters surrounding the islands. At some points (notably the pebbly beaches around the north and eastern coasts of Kefaloniá) the view from the water over to Itháki or Lefkáda is stunning.

Snorkelling and diving. The coasts around Zákynthos and Kefaloniá are a divers' paradise – the rocky shoreline is home to wide variety of creatures, and the calm, clear water gives visibility up to 50m (165ft). All scuba-diving schools have qualified instructors who will choose dive locations according to your experience. Extended boat trips are available for advanced divers. For the more advanced trips, or to hire

A thrilling boat ride along Melissáni cave lake

Boat hire

Hiring a small (25 horse-power) motorboat is the best way to explore secluded and otherwise inaccessible bays. They are available from travel agents in many places (particularly on Kefaloniá) and cost 350–80 per day plus petrol. They are great for swimming from – simply anchor, then dive or jump off the side; all boats have a fold-down ladder to help you get back on board.

equipment and go by yourself, you will need to show a diving certificate. Most major resorts have reputable diving schools. Well-reputed dive centres approved by the Professional Association of Diving Instructors (PADI; www.padi.com) include Diving Center Turtle Beach at Límni Kerioú (tel: 26950 49424; www.diving-center-turtle-beach.com), on Zákynthos, and Aquatic World in Agía Efimía (tel: 26740 62006; www.aquatic.gr), on Kefaloniá. If you don't want to indulge in full-scale scuba diving, snorkelling with simply a mask, snorkel and flippers can be equally rewarding.

Water sports. Zákynthos is the best island to visit for organised water sports, with major centres located at Tsiliví, Alykés and Ágios Nikólaos on the Vasilikós Peninsula. Boards and sails for windsurfing are available for hire at certain beaches and instruction is offered at many places. Parasailing, which is now very popular, is available at a number of beaches, mostly on Zákynthos, as is jet-skiing.

Walking

The islands not only have wonderful coasts but also beautiful interiors, much of them mountainous. There is some superb walking here and not all of it strenuous. The goal of more serious hikers will be the summit of Mount Énos (the highest peak in the Ionians), best tackled from the saddle between it and Mount Roúdi. For gentler self-guided walks log on to the Friends of the Ionian site www.foi.org.uk to download very informative walks leaflets (to access this information you will have to join the organisation and make a small donation). There are also companies that conduct walking tours of the islands, for interesting trips to Kefaloniá contact Sea Trek Adventures (tel: 01386 848814; www.sea-trek.co.uk). Serious botanists will find the hills of the islands a delight, and there are tailor-made botanical walking holidays available.

Horse Riding and Cycling

These are both excellent ways of seeing the islands. On Kefaloniá the Bavarian Horse Riding Stables, in Koulouráta about 6km (4 miles) south of Sámi, offers trips from one to seven days on horseback into the mountains and along the coast (tel: 6977 533203; www.kephalonia.com). The mountainous nature of the terrain makes cycling hard work but

The waters around Zákynthos and Kefaloniá attract yachting enthusiasts extremely rewarding. Many of the minor roads are very quiet but take great care on the precipitous main coast roads.

Excursions by Kaïki

Popular boat trips on Zákynthos are to the Blue Caves at Cape Skinári (take the *kaïki* from the lighthouse at the cape, ignoring the touts at Ágios Nikólaos) and to Navágio Beach. There are also turtle-spotting trips around Laganás Bay; Earth, Sea and Sky (www.earthseasky.org) run the most environmentally sensitive trips.

Environmental Volunteers

One of the most satisfying ways of seeing the islands is to volunteer on an environmental protection programme run by one of the local eco-groups. On Zákynthos much of the work is dedicated to safeguarding the nesting loggerhead turtles on Laganás Bay and to protecting the environment of the National Marine Park.

Yachting

The relatively calm and safe waters around Zákynthos and Kefaloniá, coupled with the wonderful marine environment, have made this area very popular with yacht owners and companies running bareboat charter and flotilla holidays. On Kefaloniá the most popular harbour is Fiskárdo in the north of the island. However, this can get very busy, especially with novice crews being instructed through loudhailers by their group leader on the quayside. If you are after a little more peace and quiet then you would be better advised to head down the coast to Agía Efimía or along the spectacular west coast to the pretty horseshoe harbour of Ássos. Companies that charter boats and run flotillas include Sunsail (www.sunsail.com) and Nautilus (www.flotillasailing.co.uk). For something a little different, check out www.ionian-seafaris.com.

Several organisations are involved in this; the park authority itself is setting up a voluntary scheme (see their website www.nmp-zak.org for details), but the longest-standing organisations on Zákynthos are the Sea Turtle Protection Society of Greece (www.archelon.gr) and Earth, Sea and Sky (www.earthseasky.org). Both run turtle protection programmes, while Earth, Sea and Sky organise other activities such as litter collection and fire prevention.

On Kefaloniá, visitors under 25 years old can apply to take part in FNEC's (Fiskárdo's Nautical and Environmental Club; www.fnec.gr) environmental protection programmes. As well as carrying out marine research work, they also run a network of volunteers to protect the feral ponies of Mount Énos.

Take a boat trip to Navágio Beach

SHOPPING

Prices are rising in Greece, and as a result you shouldn't expect great bargains on either Zákynthos or Kefaloniá. In souvenir and gift shops you might find that some good-natured bargaining is tolerated if you are buying more than one item or spending a reasonable amount, but don't push your luck. Local profit margins have to cover not only the

Shopping in Argostóli's Lithóstroto

tourist months but also the off season, when most shops are closed.

If you are not a resident of the EU, you might be able to claim back the 23 percent VAT (sales tax) included in the price of most goods, if you spend over a certain amount. Ask for details at shops with 'Tax-Free for Tourists' stickers.

What to Buy

Truth be told, Zákynthos and Kefaloniá are not a shoppers' paradise and the best things to buy as gifts or mementos of your trip are perishables, such as olive oil, thyme honey and local wines (see page 101). Among the tourist merchandise peddled in the resorts, from inflatable turtles and novelty key rings to mass-produced figurines, you'll have to look hard to find anything worth bringing home. An exception to this is jewellery, in gold and silver, which can be of very good quality and made in attractive, unusual designs. Zákynthos Town is a good place to look: try either Savvas (tel: 26950 23688) or Platinum (tel: 26950 25044), both of which are on Platía Agíou Márkou. In Argostóli most of the jewellers are along Lithóstroto. Note that the more upmarket the resort (for example, Fiskárdo), the more inflated the price of the jewellery is likely to be.

Another item worth looking out for is a decent reproduction icon. These can be skilfully executed and are widely available, but the best ones tend to be on sale at museums and monasteries.

Leather items, especially bags and sandals, can be good buys but you might want to shop around for the best quality and selection.

Ceramics are among the few artisanal items worth bringing home and the islands have some excellent craft potters, particularly in the attractive smaller villages. You may also consider buying hand-embroidered textiles; the women's cooperative in Volímes, Zákynthos, has an excellent reputation.

NIGHTLIFE

There are considerable differences in the nightlife on the two islands. For the most part, nightlife on Zákynthos falls into two broad types: that which is more traditionally Greek, ranging from the authentic (*kandádes* evenings in tavernas; see page 14) to the heavily tourist-orientated ('Greek nights'), and that revolving around the clubs in the resorts.

Dining out in Fiskárdo

If the latter is your thing, then head for Laganás on Zákynthos, which has many nightclubs, including Rescue Club, Greece's largest club outside Athens. Other places to check out include Zeros and the Cameo Club, which is on the small island of Ágios Sóstis, accessible across a walkway from the beach. Elsewhere on Zákynthos, the clubs outside Argási are pretty lively, while those in Tsiliví and Alykés are a little more staid.

A more cultural excursion on Zákynthos would be a nighttime trip to catch a performance at the Théatro Avoúri in the Skaliá Cultural Centre (see page 37).

Kefaloniá's nightlife is generally more low key and, in Argostóli, revolves around the cafés and bars on Platía Valiánou and Lithóstroto, while Pub Old House, two blocks north of the square, is a legendary laid-back rock bar and the only two proper clubs are Bass and Sin City. Elsewhere on the island, apart from in the more lively resorts of Lássi and Skála, nightlife is focused on local bars or tavernas.

Greek Nights

Whichever resort you are staying in on Zákynthos, you will almost certainly come across a 'Greek Night', which generally comprises a fairly traditional meal, music (usually live) and dancing. It is, of course, the last that everyone comes to see. Traditional Greek dances are taught at an early age, and the dancers – be they specially hired performers, restaurant staff or simply locals who want to do their bit – can almost always be relied on for an energetic performance.

Whereas some Greek island dances are a little staid, Zakynthian males revel in athletic, fast dances with high-kicking, Cossack-like steps and not a little bravado. Dancing in a ring of fire is quite typical. Another dance involves picking up a glass of wine with the mouth (no hands allowed)

A musician plays a handmade *bouzoúki*

from a press-up position. The wine is downed with a jerk of the neck. Another crowd pleaser is the solo *zimbékikos*. The spectators, clapping in time to the music, cheer on the dance. By the end of the night, it is a fair bet that the dancers will have cajoled everyone up on to the floor to join in a version of the *syrtáki*, Greece's best-known group dance; the steps are simplified for visitors.

These dances are usually all accompanied by the famous eight-stringed lute, the *bouzoúki*, which for many foreigners has become synonymous with all Greek music. In fact, the instrument (which is of Middle Eastern origin) is a comparatively recent import to the island, though made an intrinsic part of Greek folklore through the haunting melodies of Manos Hadjidakis and Mikis Theodorakis (the latter Greece's most famous modern composer, forever linked to the music he composed for the 1964 movie *Zorba the Greek*, starring Anthony Quinn in the eponymous role).

Beach-based activities are a hit with the kids

CHILDREN

It is easy to travel with a family in Greece, and Zákynthos in particular is a popular destination for those with children. The Greeks are very tolerant of children – it is common to see local youngsters late at night in tavernas, eating and running around, and visitors' children will be accepted doing the same. In addition, many of the larger and more expensive hotels and resorts have facilities for children, including play areas and dedicated, shallow swimming pools.

Many of the activities already mentioned are suitable for children and the active, outdoor life should appeal greatly to those with an adventurous spirit, with the beach being the obvious focus of activities. Do remember, however, that the Mediterranean sun is very strong and that children can burn easily and quickly. Make sure they wear a T-shirt and use a high-factor sunscreen.

On Zákynthos there are two 'toy trains' that might appeal to children. One runs frequently to and from Zákynthos Town to Argási, and another goes from Alykés in a circle through the nearby countryside, passing through Katastári and Pigadákia. Trekking on horseback is also a possibility (see page 87), though this is not one for very young children.

Activities centred around wildlife can also be popular. Trips to see the turtles (see page 88) and visits to the two natural history museums (see pages 37 and 74) are possible excursions that will go down well with the kids.

Calendar of Events

1 January New Year's Day *(Protohroniá)*. Feast Day of Ágios Vasílis (St Basil). Before Western ideas of Santa Claus became widespread in Greece, this was the traditional day on which gifts were exchanged. Children go from house to house singing the traditional *kálanda*.

6 January Epiphany *(Agía Theofánia or Fóta)*. In seaside parishes the priest or bishop blesses the waters by throwing a crucifix into the sea, then young men dive to retrieve it.

Easter The great festival of the Greek year. A moveable feast comprising several parts: **February**, *Apókries*, the period before Lent that is Greece's carnival season; **Clean Monday**, the first day of Orthodox Lent *(Katharí Deftéra)*, when in good weather everyone goes out for a picnic; **Good Friday**, biers *(epitáfii)* from many churches are taken on a procession; **Easter Sunday**, at midnight on the Saturday the priest announces *Hristós Anésti* (Christ has risen) and passes the flame of life from the altar to the candles of the congregation. There then follow fireworks and noisy celebrations with music and dance.

25 March Independence Day.

1 May May Day. Workers' parades and excursions to the countryside to gather flowers and greenery for May wreaths.

3 May Feast of Agía Mávra, Maherádo, Zákynthos.

21 May Ionian Union Day *(Énosis ton Eptaníson)* marks the anniversary of the seven islands joining the modern Greek state in 1864.

15 August Assumption of the Virgin Mary *(Apokímisis tis Panagías)*, celebrated most bizarrely in the village of Markópoulo, Kefaloniá, by a 'snake festival' (6–15 August).

16 August Feast day of Ágios Gerásimos, patron saint of Kefaloniá (also 20 October).

24 August Feast day of Ágios Dionýsios (patron saint of the island), Zákynthos Town (also 17 December).

28 October *Óhi* Day. Celebration of the Greek refusal in 1941 to accept Mussolini's ultimatum, triggering their heroic resistance of Italy's invasion.

25 December Christmas Day.

EATING OUT

In general, Greek food is delicious, fresh and well prepared. Traditionally, a restaurant *(estiatório)* does not have entertainment; it is a place for straightforward eating. These often provide *magireftá*, oven-cooked dishes that you choose by entering the kitchen and indicating what you want. Tavernas, traditionally open only at night and are more social establishments where customers may spend an entire evening drinking and eating; *psarotavérnes* specialise in fish and seafood. A *psistariá* has rotary and flat grills for cooking meats and poultry.

Mezédes and Salads

Mezédes are small plates of food, akin to starters. They can be used in combination to make up whole meals. Common *mezédes* include: olives; *tzatzíki* (yoghurt dip flavoured with garlic, cucumber and mint); *taramosaláta* (fish-roe paste blended with breadcrumbs); *melitzanosaláta* (aubergine salad); *gígandes* (broad beans in tomato sauce); and *dolmádes* (vine leaves stuffed with rice and spices). *Kalamarákia tiganitá* are pieces of deep-fried squid (this is usually frozen, not fresh); *tyropitákia* are small pastry parcels filled with cheese; *keftédes*

Some like it hot

Greek food is served lukewarm and with lots of olive oil, thought of as good for the digestion. For hot food, ask for it *zestó*; food without oil is *horís ládi*. However, both these requests will be considered eccentric.

are small, fried meatballs flavoured with coriander and spices; and *saganáki* is a slice of cheese coated in flour and fried. The standard Greek salad of tomato, cucumber, pepper, olives and feta cheese *(horiátiki saláta)* is a fine staple. *Maroúli* is lettuce, at its best as a finely shredded

Zákynthos beach bar

salad with spring onions and dill. Also popular, are various cold or lukewarm salads of boiled wild greens *(hórta)*.

Main Courses

Common dishes include *mousakás* (minced meat, aubergine and tomato with béchamel sauce and a cheese topping), brought to Greece by refugees from Asia Minor, and *pastítsio* (macaroni and minced meat with béchamel sauce). *Kléftiko* is lamb, slowly baked until it is very tender, and *stifádo* is braised beef or rabbit with pearl onions. *Briám* (potatoes, tomatoes and courgettes) and *fasolákia laderá* (green beans and tomato sauce) are two other popular casserole dishes, while *fasoláda* (bean soup) is a winter favourite. A treat, if you can find them, are *angináres* (artichokes); *bámies* (okra) are also particularly good.

Meats grilled on a small skewer are known as *souvláki*, while *gýros* are thin slices of meat cut from a spit and

Souvláki, a Greek classic

served with salad on pitta bread. *Biftéki*, fried minced meat mixed with bread and spices, is ubiquitous. *Giouvétsi* is beef or lamb, pasta and tomato cooked in a pot. *Soutzoukákia* are rolls of minced meat cooked in tomato sauce. *Giouvarlákia* are rolls of minced meat covered in egg-and-lemon sauce (*avgolémono*). For more unusual foods you may encounter *kokorétsi* (lamb's offal wrapped in intestines and grilled over a spit), *myaló* (fried sheep brains), or sheep testicles, known as 'unmentionables' (*amelétita*). *Pátsas* is tripe, served up in a spicy soup, much vaunted as a hangover cure. If you are in Greece at Easter, try the tasty *magirítsa*, a soup made from finely chopped lamb's offal.

Desserts are not usually on the menu but often offered on the house with the bill: those you are most likely to encounter include yoghurt with honey, often with walnuts, and two kinds of *halvá*. *Halvá tis rínas* is a semolina cake and the compact *halvá tou bakáli*, the grocer's *halvá*, is made of flour, tahini, oil, honey and nuts. Sometimes you will find *galaktoboúreko*, filo pastry filled with custard and soaked in syrup, and *baklavás*, made of crushed nuts in filo pastry with syrup. In the summer, particularly late summer, don't miss the abundant grapes, figs, melon and watermelon.

Local Dishes

There are a number of specialities that come from the two islands, some of which bear testimony to their history of invasion and occupation. On Zákynthos there is a strong tradition of home jam-making (known as *marmeláda*, from the English marmalade), although you will be lucky to find any outside of private houses. There is much influence from Italy across the Ionians, and this is seen in dishes such as *sofríto*, lightly fried veal with garlic and vinegar; *bourthíto*, a peppered fish stew; *biánco*, white fish stew with garlic; and *pastitsáda*, a spicy meat, macaroni and cheese dish. *Pantséta*, found on Zákynthos, is very similar to the Italian cured pork pancetta.

Kefaloniá has its *kreatópita*, a pie consisting of meat and rice flavoured with cinnamon and topped with a thick pastry. This is available almost everywhere, while rather more unusual is the octopus pie traditionally eaten during Lent. You may also

Psarotavérnes

These can be very expensive but will have some fresh fish unless winds have kept the boats in harbour. Fresh fish is sold by weight (before it is cleaned) and you might want to keep an eye on the scales, also look out for fish marked *katapsygméno* (frozen), sometimes just 'kat' or 'k'. Fish sizes vary from the tiny whitebait *(marídes)* and smelt *(atherína)*, to the larger dentex *(synagrída)*, swordfish *(xifías)* or grouper *(rofís)*. In between are the smaller red mullet *(barboúni* or *koutsomoúra)* and several breams *(tsipoúra, fangrí, sargós* and *lithríni)*. Cod *(bakaliáros)*, salted or fresh, as well as *galéos*, a kind of shark, is common. Grilled octopus *(htapódi)* and cuttlefish *(soupiá)* are delicious, and deep fried squid *(kalamarákia)*, usually frozen, is often available. You may also find lobster *(astakós)*, usually boiled, but sometimes cooked with spaghetti.

Thyme honey from Kefaloniá

come across boiled goats' meat on Kefaloniá.

An Ionian quirk is *aliáda*, essentially the same as the garlic purée found elsewhere in Greece (where it is known as *skordaliá*) but made with potatoes rather than bread. Also look out for delicious, local *kolokythákia* (courgettes) boiled whole and served with vinegar. Local cheeses are worth trying anywhere, and those made from sheep's milk are often excellent, though many of the harder ones can be very strong and salty.

Both islands have excellent thyme honey, sold by the wayside in large jars, but this is not the only sweet speciality. Zákynthos produces a very sweet nougat called *mandoláto*, made from almonds and honey. *Amygdalópita* (almond pie) is a speciality of Kefaloniá, where you will also find *kydonópasto*, a quince paste similar to the Spanish *membrillo*.

What to Drink

In the summer you will need to drink a lot of water, but do try to steer clear of bottled 'spring' water, as Greece's mountain of plastic bottles is growing ever higher. Tap water is perfectly safe on both Zákynthos and Kefaloniá, though it is extremely hard. If you carry your own water bottle, cafés and restaurants you visit will be happy to fill it for you. Better still, find one of the islands' well-regarded springs, from which locals often take their own drinking water.

Greece has delicious bottled fizzy lemonade *(lemonáda)*, which, unlike some other 'lemon drinks', does actually contain lemon juice; the best brands are Loux and IVI (HBH). Another drink worth looking out for is *soumáda*, a diluted orgeat syrup made from barley and almonds. Beer is widely available, the most likely offerings being Amstel and the more palatable Heineken; however, the local brand, Mythos, produced by the Boutari company, is one of the best.

Greece has been making wine for millennia and, although in the past some of its wines have been particularly esteemed, few are now well known outside the country. Kefaloniá is one of the best wine-producing islands and is particularly noted for whites made from the Robola grape, given an Apellation of Superior Quality. The vines grow well in the dry, stony soils common on the island, and it is possible to visit a number of the best wineries (see pages 63–66). Other major grape varieties include Muscat, used for a very fine sweet wine, and Mavrodaphne, which produces a strong red. Zákynthos also has a few good wines (see page 35), and its own cultivar, Zakynthino.

Local barrelled wines can be surprisingly good and are always worth a try. Resinated wine *(retsína)* can also be good, particularly when served very cold. *Oúzo*, a grape distillate with added aniseed oil, is drunk as an aperitif with water. *Tsípouro* is a clear, fiery grape distillate similar to the Italian *grappa*.

Wine from the Robola grape

Horiátiki, the classic Greek salad

TO HELP YOU ORDER...

Is there a table available, please?	**Ypárhi éna trapézi eléfthero, parakaló?**
I'd like a/some…	**Tha íthela éna, mía/meriká…**
The bill, please.	**To logariasmó, parakaló.**

Basic Foods

aláti	salt
avgá	eggs
kremídia	onions
ládi	(olive) oil
makarónia	pasta
méli	honey
pipéri	pepper
psomí	bread
rýzi	rice
skórdo	garlic

tyrí	cheese
voútyro	butter
xýdi	vinegar
giaoúrti	yoghurt
záhari	sugar

Mezédes

andzoúyes	anchovies
dolmádes	stuffed vine-leaves
eliés	olives

fáva	split peas
kolokithákia tiganitá	fried courgettes
loukánika	sausages
melitzánes tiganités	fried aubergines
saganáki	fried cheese
spanakópita	spinach pie
taramosaláta	fish-roe dip
tyropitákia	cheese pies
tzatzíki	yoghurt with garlic

Meat

arní	lamb
biftéki	minced meat cake
brizóla	chop
hirinó	pork
keftédes	meatballs
kotópoulo	chicken
kréas	meat
moshári	veal/beef
sta kárvouna	grilled
sto foúrno	roast
soutzoukákia	meatballs
souvláki	spit-roast

Fish

bakaliáros	salt cod
barboúnia	red mullet
frésko	fresh
garídes	prawns
htapódi	octopus
kalamarákia	squid
katapsygméno	frozen
marídes	whitebait
mýdia	mussels
psári	fish
sardéles	sardines
soupyés	cuttlefish
xifías	swordfish

Fruit and Vegetables

angináres	artichokes
arakás	peas
domátes gemistés	stuffed tomatoes
fasólia	haricot beans
hórta	greens
horiátiki	'Greek salad'
kolokithákia	courgettes
karpoúzi	watermelon
maroúli	lettuce
lemóni	lemon
patátes (tiganités/ sto foúrno)	potatoes (fried/ roast)
piperiés yemistés	stuffed peppers
portokáli	orange
saláta	salad
stafýlia	grapes
sýka	figs
veríkoka	apricot

PLACES TO EAT

The following prices reflect the average cost of a two-course meal (per person) and a half litre of wine. At all restaurants an automatic tax of 23 percent (VAT) is always included in the prices listed on the menu. It is customary to leave an additional five to 10 percent for the waiter, especially if they are an employee and not the owner.

€€€   over 28 euros
€€   17–28 euros
€   below 17 euros

ZÁKYNTHOS

ZÁKYNTHOS TOWN

Akrotiri Taverna €€ *Akrotíri, 4km (2.5 miles) north of Zákynthos Town, tel: 26950 45712.* A pleasant summer-only taverna with a large garden. Grilled meats are a speciality but staff also bring round large trays of tempting *mezédes* from which you pick and choose. Prices are reasonable, and the house wine is more than acceptable.

I Padella € *Dessylá 15, tel:26950 23356.* Just two blocks south of Platía Solomoú, this simple estiatório serves fine homestyle cooking such as pastítsio and briám in a welcoming environment.

Komis €€–€€€ *Bastoúni tou Agíou, tel: 26950 26915.* A lovely psarotavérna tucked into a rather unlikely spot behind the port authority building (opposite Agíou Dionysíou). The emphasis is on slightly pricey but fresh and inventive fish and seafood dishes, but there is a good list of *mezédes*, good wine and, better still, tempting desserts.

Malanos € *Agíou Athanasíou 38, Kípi district (south of the river off Kalamáki road), tel: 26950 45936.* A deservedly popular and inexpensive all-year shrine of *magireftá*, mince-rich *youvarlákia* and *fasolákia yahní* are typical offerings. There's also unusually good bread as well as the expected barrel wine. Often has live *kandádes* at weekends.

VASILIKÓS AND LAGANÁS BAY

Agnandi Taverna €€ *beyond Argási, 8km (5 miles) from Zákynthos Town, tel: 26950 35183.* An attractive modern wooden building on a steep slope overlooking the sea. It is slightly touristy, but the home cooking is authentic and tasty. The menu covers the generic standards, but also has some interesting specials.

Apelati € *1km (0.5 miles) east of Kerí, tel: 26950 43324.* This lovely rural tavern, tucked behind a field off the main road, offers a simple selection of wholesome country dishes from fresh meat and fish to delicious salads, much of it made from home produce.

Dennis €€ *Lithákia, tel: 26950 51387.* A bit of an institution, and open all year round, Dennis's is a friendly, family-run long-standing taverna with a great atmosphere, serving a wide range of traditional food. Try the *mezédes* and meat from the charcoal grill – the pork chops are legendary; the house wine isn't bad either. There is also free transport back to your villa or hotel should you need it.

Sarakina €€ *2km (1.2 miles) west of Laganás, tel: 26950 51606.* Set in a rambling old house with outdoor terraces amidst the olive groves, this evening-only taverna offers a huge range of quality local food and wine, as well as traditional music, popular with Greeks and tourists alike. It is well-advertised in Laganás and a free minibus comes round regularly to shuttle diners back and forth.

Theodoritsis €€–€€€ *just past Argási in Vasilikós municipal territory, tel: 26950 48500.* Theodoritsis is where the beau monde of Zákynthos go for a weekend blowout; the stress is on *magireftá*, but grills and *mezédes* are also available. Moderately pricey. Summer terrace overlooking town and tasteful interior. Open all year.

To Fanari tou Keriou €€–€€€ *1.5 km (1 mile) beyond Kerí village, on southwest tip of island, tel: 26950 43384.* Worth the trip out, especially on nights when you can watch the full moon rise over the sea-stacks known as the Myzíthres. The food's on the expensive side, but portions are fair size and quality is high – try vegetable-stuffed *pandséta*, redolent of nutmeg, and daily-made *galaktoboúreko*. Reservations essential.

To Triodi €€ *Gérakas, tel:26950 35215.* Lovely garden taverna next door to the Turtle Information Centre, where you can enjoy a variety of filling meat and fish dishes or smaller salads and snacks before a dip at the fantastic beach.

Zakanthi €€ *Kalamáki, tel: 26950 43586.* This is probably the most attractive place to eat in Kalamáki, with dining in a large well-maintained garden. The food, which is quite good, is a mix of pasta, pizza and the usual Greek offerings (grills and salads). Once the sun has gone down and the subdued lighting comes on in the garden, it is lovely here.

THE NORTH

Alitzerini €€ *entrance to Kiliómeno, tel: 26950 48552.* Housed in one of the few surviving 17th-century Venetian village houses, this little *inomagirío* offers hearty, meat-based country cooking and (as ever) its own wine; *kandádes* some evenings. Evenings only: Fri–Sun Oct–May, daily June–Sept. Reservations essential. During the day, head for **Korfiatos**, a wooden balcony at the top of the hill with lovely views. Here you can have a drink or simple meal. Behind the benches are huge barrels of local wine, as well as excellent local oil and thyme honey for sale.

Kaki Rahi €–€€ *Pigadákia, 26950 63670.* In one of the nicer inland settings on the island. A decent range of *magireflá*, grills and *mezédes* are served on a leafy terrace beside a running stream from which the taverna gets its name. The local wine served here is excellent too.

Kalas €–€€ *Kambí, in the village before the road climbs up to the headland, no tel.* Kalas is by far the best taverna in Kambí – the others, located on the headland, serve substandard food to coachloads of tourists bussed in to see the sunset. Kalas is set in a pretty garden, shaded by large trees, and serves up all the usual favourites (*fáva*, *loukánika*, *horiátiki* and *patátes*), but all are tasty and freshly cooked. Good bulk wine as well.

Mikro Nisi €€ *Kokkínos, 1km (0.6 miles) beyond Makrýs Gialós, tel: 26950 31566.* Standard, but reasonable, taverna food – *horiátiki*, *kalamarákia*, *souvláki* and the like – but served in a delightful setting. The taverna is perched on the edge of a small headland overlooking a tiny harbour and you can watch the boats bobbing in the inlet as you eat.

Porto Limnionas €–€€ *Pórto Limniónas, near Ágios Léon, 26950 48650.* Location can count for a lot, and this restaurant has one of the best on the island. The food is reasonably-priced, standard taverna fare, plus some less common *mezédes* and pricier fish dishes, all served on a promontory overlooking an idyllic rocky bay. To cap things off, the restaurant faces west, so is a great place to watch the sun set.

Rouli's €–€€ *Kypséli Beach, near Drosiá, tel: 26950 61628.* A friendly place overlooking the sea and a narrow beach – and popular with islanders – Rouli's gets very fresh fish (one of its main attractions) but also has a good line in the usual Greek salads and vegetables. The house wine is drinkable, and the freshness of all the ingredients make a trip here well worth the detour off the main road.

KEFALONIÁ

ARGOSTÓLI

There are a few places on or just off Platía Vallianoú that are good for breakfast, a snack or for simply sitting with a drink. **Premiere**, between Hotel Aenos and the Ionian Plaza, advertises itself as a *crêperie-gelaterie* but is not a bad place for breakfast (even if the service is very slow). Better is **Siora Kate**, just up the hill at K. Vergóti 9, a small but popular bakery serving tasty savoury pies and *bougátsa* (usually in the form of a creamy custard pastry served warm). Of the cafés surrounding the square, the **Central Café** (tel: 26710 26680), on the corner near the Foká-Kosmetátou Foundation, is one of the most pleasant.

Captain's Table €€–€€€ *Rizospáston, tel: 26710 23896.* Captain Makis has been serving his own delicious versions of traditional Greek dishes for 19 years. An attractive and friendly taverna decorated in 1950s nautical style, with live *kandádes* on Saturday and every night in the season. There is a quieter second location on the seafront.

Kyani Akti €€ *A. Trítsi 1, far north end of the quay, tel: 26710 26680.* A superb *psarotavérna* built out over the sea. The speciality is, unsurprisingly, fresh fish and seafood, and they often have unusual things to try (including sea urchins and the delicious *dáktylia* – 'fingers' – which are akin to razor clams). All the fish and seafood is sold by weight (you go and pick it from the buckets at the back), but there is also a range of meat, *mezédes* and salads, plus tasty house wine.

Maïstrato €–€€ *far north end of quay by fishing anchorage, tel: 26710 26563.* Set yourself up at this genuine *ouzerí* with a seafood *pikilía* (medley), some of their abundant hot/cold *mezédes* and *oúzo* by the 200-ml carafe. Very reasonable, pleasant waterside seating beside a pine grove (take mosquito repellent, as these insects can be quite fierce here). Apr–Oct only.

Patsouras € *Lavrága, tel: 26710 22779.* Popular *magireftá* specialist in new premises in between the main square and the seafront. Good ribsticking food, with especially tasty *bámies* (okra), a few grills and big portions, and there is velvety red house wine. It's open all year.

To Arhondiko €–€€ *Rizospáston 5, tel: 26710 27213.* This compact, friendly taverna has seating on a small outside patio, from which you can hear the *kandádes* sung at the adjacent Captain's Table, whilst paying considerably less for tasty fare such as *exohikó* (baked lamb) or veal in tomato sauce. The *mezédes* and wine are excellent too.

To Kafenio tis Kabanas € *Lithóstroto 52B, tel: 26710 24456.*
Housed in a reconstructed Venetian tower and with seating in the
square opposite, this pleasant café serves light snacks. Run by the
local ROTA cooperative, it helps place people with mental-health
problems back in jobs and the community. As well as the usual
run of coffees there are a few local specialities, such as *soumáda*
(an orgeat drink) and *amygdalópita* (almond pie).

LIXOÚRI AND THE SOUTH

Akrogiali € *Lixoúri quay (Andréa Laskarátou), towards south end,
tel: 26710 92613.* An enduring, budget-priced institution, with
largely local clientele. Wholesome and tasty food with a stress
on oven-casserole food (including *giouvétsi*, *kreatópita* and great
hórta), but also fish and grills in the evening, plus excellent bulk
wine.

Blue Sea (aka Spyros') €€–€€€ *Káto Katélios, tel: 26710 81353.*
The speciality here is pricey, but fresh and superbly grilled, fish
from the little anchorage adjacent. Budget on about €30 each for
a large portion with a share of *mezédes* and their bulk wine. Credit
cards are accepted.

Paspalis €–€€ *Skála, tel: 26710 83140.* Lively by day and night,
this beachside restaurant is one of the best in the resort for authentic homestyle cooking such as *mousakás* and g*iouvétsi*. Pricier
fish is also available.

Romantza (aka Fotis Family) €–€€ *Póros, southern end of the
town beach, tel: 26740 72294.* This estiatório is in a delightful position, built into the headland at the end of the town beach. You eat
on a first-storey balcony, which has views over the sea to Itháki.
The focus of the menu is on a large range of fresh fish (priced by
weight), but there are also good *mezédes* and salads.

Ta Delfinia €–€€ *Sámi waterfront, tel: 26740 22008.* A basic
but pleasant waterfront place with daily *magireftá* such as *briám*
(similar to ratatouille), *giouvétsi* and good *hórta*. There is also
some fresh fish, usually small tasty offerings including sardines,

octopus and *marídes*. This is about the best in a line of rather touristy places, all with outdoor seating overlooking the harbour.

Xouras €–€€ *Petaní, Lixoúri peninsula, tel: 26710 97128.* Slap bang in the middle of one of the island's best beaches and run by a welcoming Greek-American woman, this is a great spot for sunset dining. Grills and fish are the specialities, as well as salads and some *magireftá*.

THE NORTH

Agia Paraskevi €€ *Agía Paraskeví, between Sámi and Agía Efimía, tel: 26740 23061.* A lovely spot from which to watch the waves break on the rocks below the huge terrace. The standard range of salads, *mezédes* and grilled meat and fish is available but the real speciality is the superb seafood marinara, bulging with fresh mussels and shrimp. You can dance it off in the adjacent Del Mare nightclub.

Lagoudera €–€€ *Fiskárdo, tel: 26740 41275.* Authentic restaurant with one branch on the harbour of Fiskárdo, the other just around the corner by the small square. Specialities include tasty home-style baked food, as well as fish, grilled meat and all the usual mezédes. Open Apr–Oct.

Makis € *Vasilikiádes, tel: 26740 51556.* You can enjoy a wonderful, inexpensive and extremely authentic meal in the large courtyard of this inland village establishment. There are succulent grills like lamb chops, as well as fine *mezédes* such as *kolokythokeftedes* (cheesy courgette patties).

Nefeli-Anait €€ *Ássos, tel: 26740 51251.* One of four establishments overlooking the very attractive harbour, this all-purpose taverna offers the usual range of salads and a few grilled and oven dishes, as well as fresh fish by the kilo. There is good barrelled wine and a selection of other drinks. If this place is too crowded, try the **Estiatorio Platanos** on Platía Parísion behind the waterfront, set around a large tree; this second restaurant is popular with visiting Greeks and has a huge range of reasonable food.

Odisseas €–€€ *Agía Ierousalím, tel: 26740 41133.* A true hidden gem. You are assured a warm welcome and relaxed dining experience from the brother-and-sister duo who run this place. All their ingredients are organic or free range and you can sample delights such as olive bread, slow-cooked lamb and ultra-fresh salads, all washed down with the fine house wine. They also have home-made honey, jam and other produce for sale.

Paradisenia Akti (Stavros Dendrinos) €€ *far east corner of Agía Efimía resort, above 'Paradise Beach', tel: 26740 61392.* Fair-priced, savoury dishes such as *hortópita* and local sausage, though the sea-food portions could be bigger; lovely terrace seating under pines and grape arbours, overlooking the sea.

To Foki € *at the head of Fókis Bay, tel: 6944 757032.* This is a very pleasant taverna, friendly and just opposite the beach. It serves simple but tasty food – *fáva, souvláki* and salads – and lovely *milópita* (apple pie). Much better, and far cheaper, than anything to be found in Fiskárdo just down the road. Take mosquito repellent for the evenings.

To Pefko €€ *Andipáta Erísou, just by the turning for Dafnoúdi beach, tel: 26740 41360.* A serious contender for the best place to eat on the island. The seating is outside under a huge pine tree, which becomes nicely atmospheric at dusk. The women in the kitchen are geniuses, cooking a mouthwatering selection of *mezédes*, oven-cooked dishes and some grilled meat and fish. Particularly good are the tomato, mint and féta 'keftédes', the *gígandes* (butter beans) and aubergine with garlic. For dessert don't miss the (hot) *fýllo* covered ice cream with sour cherries. As a bonus, the beer glasses are kept in the freezer.

Vasso's €€–€€€ *southeast end of quay, Fiskárdo, tel: 06740 41276.* Ma-gireftá with a difference: olive tapenade for your bread, dill and other herbs flavour many of the dishes, and there is seafood pasta and creative desserts. Reasonable (for *Fiskárdo* anyway) at about €25 each if you stay away from lobster and other more expensive types of fish.

A–Z TRAVEL TIPS

A Summary of Practical Information

A

ACCOMMODATION

Many hotels are heavily booked from mid-June until mid-September, especially during the first three weeks of August when reservations are strongly recommended. The decline in numbers of recent years means you should find a room on spec or via a travel agency on either island. On Kefaloniá, you can ask at the Tourist Information Office in Argostóli (see under Tourist Information).

Prices are controlled according to a rating system, based on a building's age, facilities, amenities and other factors. Hotels are rated from A to E (rooms in categories A and B have private bathrooms), but prices can vary widely within each category. Luxury establishments, rated L, are not price-controlled. A star system, designed to replace the letter scheme, was introduced in 2003 but has met with resistance. The equivalents are roughly as follows:

Luxury – 5 stars
A – 4 stars
B – 3 stars
C – 2 stars
D and E – 1 star

In high summer some form of air conditioning will enable you to get a good night's sleep. If your room doesn't have air conditioning (and some older properties don't), there will either be a ceiling fan or you might be able to borrow a fan from reception or the owner.

Villas and apartments. There are many villas, apartments and studios (the latter terms are interchangeable) in Zákynthos and Kefaloniá available to rent. Accommodation ranges from simple rooms to lavishly appointed summer homes – sometimes tastefully converted from a traditional house or houses – complete with a swimming pool.

In the UK, companies specialising in top-of-the-range secluded luxury villas on Zákynthos and Kefaloniá are: Ionian & Aegean Island Holidays, tel: 020 8459 0777, www.ionianislandholidays.com; Simply Ionian, tel: 020 8541 2200, www.simplytravel.co.uk; Sunisle, tel: 0871 222 1226, www.sunisle.co.uk; and Sunvil (Greek Islands Club), tel: 020 8568 4499, www.sunvil.co.uk.

Rooms in private homes. The cheapest rooms are those that are privately rented in people's homes, but these are becoming increasingly rare. They are almost always clean, and are graded A and B by the local tourist police, though rates are usually negotiable.

I'd like a single/double room with bath/shower What's the rate per night?	**Tha íthela éna monóklino/ díklino me bánio/dous Póso éhi/stihízi gia káthe vrádi?**

AIRPORTS

Zákynthos: Located about 5km (3 miles) from Zákynthos Town, this busy airport has been recently renovated with spacious new arrivals and departures areas and improved facilities. If you book through a tour operator you will be met at the airport and whisked off to your villa or resort, otherwise you will have to take a taxi into town (around €9–10). For information on flight arrivals and departures tel: 26950 29500.

Kefaloniá: The airport is near the village of Miniá, about 7km (4 miles) south of Argostóli. The building is modern, with a few basic facilities such as a shop and refreshment stand, but like all island airports it can get very busy during high season. If you are not being met by a tour representative or are picking up a hire car booked in advance, then you have no option but to take a – costly – taxi into town (about €12–13). For information on arrivals and departures tel: 26710 29900.

B

BICYCLE AND MOTORCYCLE HIRE

You can hire bicycles, motorcycles and quad bikes in all the tourist centres. However, many package operators warn clients against motorised cycles and scooters for the quite legitimate fear of an accident (and to drum up more business for organised excursions). It is vital that you check that motorbike hire does not invalidate your holiday insurance. Scooter hire is cheap (you should be quoted a rate per day, including third-party insurance and CDW, collision-damage waiver). Terms vary by operator. Usually, to hire a motorbike with an engine larger than 50cc you must be at least 18 years old and hold a full motorcycle licence. It is illegal to ride without a crash helmet, or to drive without an appropriate licence on your person; the spot fines approach €100.

It is certainly not advisable to ride a motorbike in shorts or a swimsuit, since burns or scrapes resulting from even a slight accident could be appalling. Inspect brakes and tyres before hiring and drive with care. Even on good roads there are occasional potholes.

Bicycle hire is less common, largely because of the mountainous terrain, but on Kefaloniá a good place for serious riders to seek information is the bike shop at the far (non-pedestrianised) end of Lithóstroto.

BUDGETING FOR YOUR TRIP

Greece is certainly not a budget destination these days and particularly so since the introduction of the euro. However, it is still possible not to spend a fortune on Zákynthos and Kefaloniá, especially if you book an airfare/accommodation package. Otherwise, independent travellers can find return flights for around £150–200 decent places to stay for around €50–60 per night for a double room, with big discounts available out of the high season.

Eating out is considerably cheaper if you stick to *magireftá* and simple grills and *mezédes* in places frequented by locals: generally a three-course meal plus drinks in a decent restaurant or taverna will cost around €15–25 per person. Public transport and museum fees are inexpensive.

C

CAR HIRE

Unless visiting the islands with the intention of walking or cycling, you might consider hiring a car, especially on Zákynthos, where the bus service is very patchy. As elsewhere in Greece, car hire is not particularly cheap, but it is certainly less expensive than touring by taxi. Car hire starts from about €25 per day in low season (with a €500 excess on insurance for damage). For a decent family-sized car in high season, you should budget around €250 per week; all have air conditioning these days.

You'll find car-hire firms throughout the islands, especially in tourist centres. To be on the safe side, reserve a car ahead of time, especially for the high season. Local firms generally charge slightly less than international agencies and provide equally good cars and service. International chains that operate on the islands, bookable through their websites, include Avis, Budget, Europcar, Hertz, National, Sixt and Thrifty.

You will usually need a credit card for the deposit and a full national licence (held for at least one year) from your country of residence. If you are from a non-EU country, it is also mandatory to have an international driving permit. Depending on the model and the hire company, the minimum age for hiring a car varies from 21 to 25. Third-party liability insurance (CDW) is usually included in the

What's the hire charge for a full day?	**Póso kostízi giá mía méra?**
I'd like to hire a car (tomorrow)	**Tha íthela na nikiáso éna avtokínito (ávrio)**

stated rate, but with an excess amount, so it is always worth paying a little more for comprehensive coverage.

CLIMATE

July and August are the sunniest, hottest and busiest tourist months. You may prefer to visit between mid-May and late June or from early September to mid-October. It can rain at any time of year, even in July and August. The Ionians are the greenest of all the Greek island chains. In winter it rains very hard. November and December are the wettest months and January the coldest, but even during these mid-winter doldrums the climate is temperate. Spring, when the islands burst with wild flowers, is the best time for walking.

The chart below shows each month's average air and sea temperature in Celsius and Fahrenheit, and the average number of hours of sunshine per day.

	J	F	M	A	M	J	J	A	S	O	N	D
Air												
°C	10	10	12	15	19	24	27	26	23	19	15	12
°F	50	50	54	59	66	75	81	79	73	66	59	54
Sea												
°C	15	15	15	16	18	21	24	25	24	21	19	18
°F	59	59	59	61	64	70	75	77	75	70	66	64
Sunshine hours												
	5	6	7	7	9	10	11	12	9	6	4	3

CLOTHING

Clothing is almost always casual on the islands. However, the Greeks do like to dress up when they go out in the evening and visitors who make a bit of an effort will be smiled upon. With regard to comfort, choose lightweight cotton clothing in spring and summer, and a warm jacket, sweater and rainwear in autumn and winter. Since it rains from time to time (outside of July and August), a protective coat or umbrella might be a good idea. Plastic or 'trekking' sandals are extremely useful for stony beaches; these are usually available in some shape or form from beach-side tourist shops.

CRIME AND SAFETY (see also Emergencies and Police)

The Zakynthians and Kefalonians are, like the vast majority of Greek people, scrupulously honest. However, unfortunately, thefts occur, so it's sensible to leave valuables in the hotel safe. Take care of your passport but at the same time be aware that you're required to have official ID on your person at all times in Greece.

Possession of drugs is a very serious matter in Greece, carrying a stiff mandatory sentence. Make sure you have a prescription from your doctor if you will be carrying syringes, insulin, any narcotic drugs or even codeine, which is illegal in Greece.

D

DRIVING

Road conditions. Zákynthos has a reputation for having some of the most dangerous roads in Greece, so be very careful. The surfaces on main roads are generally very good, though curves in the road are often indicated too late, are sometimes unsignposted and are never banked. If there is a mirror on a bend, slow down to a low gear, it is probably going to be extremely tight or narrow, or perhaps both.

On many clifftop roads it is very dangerous to pass, so be patient if there is a slow-moving bus or heavy vehicle in front of you. Conversely, try to let local speed maniacs pass you as soon as it is safe to do so.

The secondary roads are some of the narrowest on any of the Greek islands – it's difficult to safely exceed 50kph (31mph) – while anything marked 'unsurfaced' on a map can be very rough indeed. Rockslides are common in the rainy season, and broken shoulders or potholes are not unknown on even the best-paved stretches. Drive with extreme caution, as you might be responsible for damage sustained to the underside of your hire car, even with comprehensive coverage.

Driving regulations. Drive on the right side and pass on the left. Traffic from the right has right of way. A Greek practice to be aware of is that if a driver flashes the lights, it means 'Stay where you are, I'm coming through', not 'Go ahead'. Seat belts are obligatory, as is the carrying of your driving licence while at the wheel; there is an €86 spot fine if you are caught without it. The speed limit is 80kph (50mph) inside built-up areas, 100kph (62mph) outside. In practice, however, the winding roads usually set the speed limit.

Are we on the right road for...?	**Eímaste sto sostó drómo gia...?**
Fill the tank please, with (unleaded) petrol	**Parakaló, gemíste tin me amólivdi**
My car has broken down	**To avtokínito mou éhi halási**
There's been an accident	**Égine éna atíhima**

Fuel. Generally you will never be far from a filling station, though in parts of the north and west of Zákynthos, and the north and centre of Kefaloniá, they are fairly few and far between. Note that in rural areas filling stations are open only until about 7pm and closed on Sunday. On busy main roads and in resorts they open daily from early until late.

If you need help. For breakdown and accident assistance phone the Greek motoring club (ELPA), tel: 104, which has a reciprocal arrangement with most other national motoring associations. Some car-hire companies have agreements with other roadside emergency companies, such as Hellas Service (tel: 157).

Road signs. On main roads and at junctions these will be in Greek and Latin (Western) letters; on secondary roads they may just be in Greek (for some important ones see the list below).

Detour	Παράκαμψη/Parákampsi
Parking	Πάρκιγκ/Párking
No parking	Απαγορεύεται το πάρκιγκ/ Apagorévete to párking
Be careful	Προσοχή/Prosohí
Bus stop	Στάση λεοφορείου/ Stási leoforíou
Pedestrians	Για πεζούς/Gia pezoús
Danger	Κίνδυνος, επικίνδυνος/ Kíndynos, epikíndynos
No entry	Απαγορεύεται η είσοδος/ Apagorévete i ísodos

E

ELECTRICITY

Greece has 220-volt/50-cycle AC current. Sockets are two-pin, so bring an adapter or transformer with you as necessary.

| a transformer | énas metashimatistís |
| an adapter | énas prosarmostís |

EMBASSIES AND CONSULATES *(presvía; proxenío)*

There is a United Kingdom consular office located in Zákynthos Town.

British Consulate: Fóskolou 5, Zákynthos Town; tel: 26950 22906.
Embassies or consulates of all major countries are located in Athens.

Australia: Level 6, Thon Building, corner Kifissías and Alexandras avenues, tel: 21087 04000, www.greece.embassy.gov.au.

Canada: Gennadíou 4, tel: 21072 73400, www.canadainternational. gc.ca/greece-grece.

Ireland: Vassiléos Konstantínou 7, tel: 21072 32771, www.embassy ofireland.gr.

New Zealand: Kifissías Avenue 76, tel: 21069 24136.

South Africa: Kifissías Avenue 60, tel: 21061 06645.

UK: Ploutárhou 1, tel: 21072 72600, http://ukingreece.fco.gov.uk.

US: Vassilísis Sofías 91, tel: 21072 12951, http://athens.usembassy.gov.

EMERGENCIES

Police: (all-purpose emergency number) **100**; (Zákynthos Town) 26950 83083; (Argostóli) 26710 22200.

Tourist Police: 171; (Zákynthos Town) 26950 24450; (Argostóli) 26710 22815.

Hospitals: (Zákynthos Town) 26950 59100/59168; (Argostóli) 26710 24641/23230.

Ambulance: 166; (Zákynthos Town) 26950 23166.

Fire: 199.

Vehicle emergency: 104 or **157**.

Port Authority: (Zákynthos Town) 26950 28117; (Argostóli) 26710 22224.

G

GETTING THERE

It is possible to cross Europe overland and take the ferry from Italy to Pátra on the Greek mainland and then a ferry to either Sámi on Kefaloniá, or, from Kyllíni, further down the coast, to Zákynthos Town. From the UK it is easier to fly into Athens (the low-cost airline easyJet, www.easyjet.com, flies to Athens from London) and then either connect for the Olympic (www.olympicair.com) internal flights to the islands (45 minutes), or take the coach from the Kifissoú bus station (several daily to Zákynthos and Argostóli, around 7 hours; all coaches connect with ferries for which there is a small additional cost).

From April to October easyJet has direct flights from London Gatwick to both islands or there are charter flights from a number of regional British airports to Zákynthos and Kefaloniá, taking around 3 hours.

H

HEALTH AND MEDICAL CARE

In theory, EU citizens with a European Health Insurance Card (obtainable in their own country) can get free treatment under the Greek health service. However, you are likely to receive the minimum treatment, must pay for medication and state hospital facilities are over-stretched in the tourist season. It's therefore preferable to obtain private medical insurance for your holiday. Doctors and dentists are concentrated in Zákynthos Town and Argostóli; your hotel or apartment owner will be able to find you one who speaks English. Most resorts have a local medical clinic.

Hospitals. The hospitals in Zákynthos Town and Argostóli operate a 24-hour emergency service (tel: 166, or, Zákynthos: tel: 26950 59100/59168; Argostóli tel: 26710 24641/23230). Otherwise call the tourist police (Zákynthos tel: 26950 27367; Argostóli tel: 26710 22815).

Pharmacies. A red or green cross on a white background identifies a pharmacy (FARMAKEIO – *farmakío*). They are normally open only during the morning Monday to Friday but a notice on the door should tell you the nearest one for after-hours service. One pharmacy

a doctor/dentist	**énas giatrós/odontogiatrós**
hospital	**nosokomío**
an upset stomach	**varystomahiá**
sunstroke	**ilíasi**
a fever	**pyretós**

is always open in Zákynthos Town and Argostóli at night and on Saturday and Sunday. Without a prescription, you can't get sleeping pills, barbiturates or medicine for stomach upsets.

While swimming look out for sea urchins – their black spines are very sharp and will break off in your skin. If this happens, seek medical attention, as they are very tricky to remove.

L

LANGUAGE

Only in remote countryside spots will non-Greek-speaking tourists run into serious communication problems. You will find that basic English is spoken almost everywhere. Stress is a very important feature of the Greek language, denoted by an accent above the vowel of the syllable to be emphasised. The table above lists the Greek letters in their upper- and lower-case forms, followed by the closest individual or combined letters to which they correspond in English.

Α	α	a	as in c**a**t
Β	β	v	as in **v**eto
Γ	γ	g	as in **g**o (except before i and e sounds, when it's like the y in **y**es)
Δ	δ	d	sounds like th in **th**is
Ε	ε	e	as in g**e**t
Ζ	ζ	z	same as in English
Η	η	i	as in sk**i**
Θ	θ	th	as in **th**in
Ι	ι	i	as in sk**i**
Κ	κ	k	same as in English
Λ	λ	l	same as in English
Μ	μ	m	same as in English

Ν	ν	n	same as in English
Ξ	ξ	x	as in bo**x**
Ο	ο	o	as in **t**o**p**
Π	π	p	same as in English
Ρ	ρ	r	similar to English, but slightly rolled
Σ	σ	s	as in ki**ss** (at start or middle of word)
	ς	s	as in ki**ss** (at end of word)
Τ	τ	t	same as in English
Υ	υ	y	as in countr**y**
Φ	φ	f	same as in English
Χ	χ	h	as in Scottish lo**ch**
Ψ	ψ	ps	as in ti**ps**y
Ω	ω	o	as in **t**o**p**

M

MAPS

The best maps available of Zákynthos and Kefaloniá are by Orama Editions. They are clear and accurate and give place names in both Greek letters and in transliteration. They are available locally from Stanfords in the UK (tel: 020 7836 1321). Free tourist maps of lesser quality are widely available.

MEDIA

Newspapers and magazines (*efimerídes; periodiká*). During the tourist season, foreign-language newspapers are on sale at shops and kiosks on the island, generally on the day after publication. The only Greek English-language paper is the Athens News (€2, every Friday).

Television (*tiliórasi*). Most hotels and many bars offer satellite television networks, including CNN, BBC World and, more rarely, Sky.

Radio. BBC World Service is no longer broadcast on short wave but can be streamed on www.bbc.co.uk.

MONEY

Currency *(nómisma)*. In common with most other Western European countries, the euro (EUR or €) is the official currency used in Greece. Notes are in denominations of 5, 10, 20, 50, 100 and 500 euros; coins are 1 and 2 euros and 1, 2, 5, 10, 20 and 50 cents.

Banks and currency exchange. You'll find banks in Zákynthos Town, Argostóli and in the larger resort areas. Hotels and travel agencies (the latter sometimes called 'tourist offices') are authorised to change money, but you will probably get less for your money than you would from a bank.

ATMs. The easiest method to obtain cash is through 'hole-in-the-wall' cash dispensers. These can be found in Zákynthos Town, Argostóli and in all of the larger resorts. Depending upon your own individual card fees, this might also be the cheapest way to get money.

Credit cards *(pistotikés kártes)*. The major credit cards are accepted in many shops and by car-hire firms, most hotels, more expensive restaurants and some (but not all) filling stations. Be aware that you might have to pay an additional 5 to 7 percent for the privilege of using plastic.

Travellers cheques. Most major brands of travellers cheques – in any Western currency – are readily cashed. Always take your passport for identification.

I want to change some pounds/dollars/ travellers cheques	**Thélo na alláxo merikés líres/meriká dollária/ taxidiotikés epitagés**
Can I pay with this credit card?	**Boró na plíróso me aftí tin pistotikí kárta?**

O

OPENING TIMES

The siesta (the traditional Mediterranean early afternoon break) is still alive and well on Zákynthos and Kefaloniá, and observed most strictly outside tourist areas.

Shops. Traditional hours are generally Mon–Sat 8.30 or 9am–2 or 2.30pm. On Tuesday, Thursday and Friday shops reopen in the evening from 5.30 or 6pm until 8.30–9pm. Shops catering to tourists often stay open through the siesta and until late each evening in the summer, as well as part of Sunday. Larger supermarkets open Mon–Fri 8.30am–8.30pm and Sat 9am–6pm.

Museums and tourist attractions. State-run museums are closed on Monday. Museums are typically open Tue–Sat 8.30am–3pm and Sun 8.30 or 9.30am–2.30 or 3pm.

Banks. Mon–Thur 8am–2.30pm and Fri 8.30am–2pm.

Businesses and offices. 8am–1pm, then 2–5pm. Government offices work 8am–1.30pm, sometimes 2.30pm, and don't reopen.

Restaurants and tavernas. More traditional establishments open for lunch from noon until around 3.30pm and for dinner from 7pm to 11.30pm or later.

P

POLICE

Emergency telephone number: **100**.
Tourist police: Zákynthos, tel: 26950 27367
Argostóli, tel: 26710 22815

The tourist police (*touristikí astynomía*) have a specific mission to help visitors to the island, as well as to accompany state inspectors of hotels and restaurants to ensure that proper standards and prices are maintained.

Traffic police check car documents and driving licences, operate speed traps and issue fines for illegal parking (fines in Greece are high). Car-hire companies will use your credit-card details to pay ignored parking tickets; you have 10 working days to pay moving violations in person. Failing that, a court date will be set, and a summons sent to your home address. Failure to appear will result in an extra conviction for contempt of court, and make future re-entry to Greece extremely difficult.

Where's the nearest police station?	**Pou íne to kondinótero astynomikó tmíma?**

POST OFFICES

Post offices (ELTA) handle letters, parcels and money orders but no longer exchange foreign currency. Look for a blue sign with the head of Hermes traced on it in yellow.

Post offices are generally open Mon–Fri 7.30am–2pm. Registered letters and parcels to non-EU destinations are checked before being sent, so don't seal them until presenting them at the desk. The main post office in Zákynthos Town is on Tertséti (Mon–Fri 7.30am–4pm), in Argostóli it is found on Lithóstroto (open as above).

Letterboxes are yellow but if there are two slots, make sure you use the one marked *exoterikó* (abroad). In tourist hotels, the receptionist will take care of dispatching your mail.

Have you received any mail for…?	**Éhete grámmata giá…?**
a stamp for this letter/ postcard	**éna grammatósimo giaftó to grámma/giaftí tin kart postál**
express (special delivery)	**katepígon**
registered	**systiméno**

PUBLIC HOLIDAYS

Banks, offices and shops are closed on the following national holidays, as well as during some feasts and festivals (see also the Calendar of Events on page 95):

1 January	*Protohroniá*	New Year's Day
6 January	*Ágia Theofánia*	Epiphany
25 March	*Ikostipémpti Martíou (tou Evangelismoú)*	Greek Independence Day
1 May	*Protomagiá*	May Day
15 August	*Dekapendávgoustos (tis Panagías)*	Assumption Day
28 October	*Ikostiogdóis Oktovríou*	*Óhi* ('No') Day, celebrating defiance of the 1940 Italian ultimatum
25 December	*Hristoúgenna*	Christmas Day
26 December	*Sýnaxi Theotókou*	Meeting of Virgin's Entourage

Moveable dates:

Katharí Deftéra	1st day of Lent: 'Clean Monday'
Megáli Paraskeví	Good Friday
Páscha	Easter
tou Agíou Pnévmatos	Whit (Pentecost) Sunday and Monday ('Holy Spirit'), June

Note: These moveable holidays are celebrated according to dates in the Greek Orthodox calendar, which often differ from Catholic or Protestant dates.

R

RELIGION

The national religion of Greece is Greek Orthodox. You must dress modestly to visit churches and monasteries, which normally means long trousers for men, a long skirt or trousers for women and covered shoulders for both sexes. However, men are often allowed to wear long shorts and skirts may be provided at the back of churches for women to wrap around themselves.

T

TELEPHONES

Local calling. There are no longer any area codes as such in Greece; even within the same local-call zone you must dial all 10 digits of the number. What were the old codes are now merely the locators: 26950 for all of Zákynthos; 26710 for Argostóli, Lixoúri and the southwest; and 26740 for the east coast and north from Póros to Fiskárdo, plus the island of Itháki.

From overseas. To call Greece from abroad, first dial the international access code (00 from the UK), then 30 (the country code for Greece) and finally all 10 digits of the local number.

Long distance from Greece. International direct dialling is available at street-corner phone booths. These take phonecards *(tilekártes)*, which are quite good value. Pre-paid VoIP calling cards with a freephone access code and scratch-off PIN number are becoming more common; they can be used from any phone and are by far the cheapest way to call abroad. To reverse charges (collect calls), dial 151 for Europe and 161 for the rest of the world. Overseas directory assistance is through the international operator (dial 161). For the local operator, dial 132.

reverse-charge (collect) call	**plirotéo apó to paralípti**

TIME ZONES

Greek time is GMT plus two hours. Daylight saving, when Greek clocks are put forward one hour, is observed from the last Sunday of March to the last Sunday of October. The chart shows the times in Greece and various other places during the European summer.

New York	London	Paris	**Greece**	Sydney	Auckland
5am	10am	11am	**noon**	8pm	9pm

TIPPING

The Greeks aren't obsessed with tipping, but it is the norm to leave a little more if service has been good. Usual amounts are as follows: hotel porter, up to €2; hotel maid, €1 per day; waiter, 5–10 percent; taxi driver, 10 percent; hairdresser/barber, 10 percent; lavatory attendant, €0.30.

TOILETS

Public conveniences are rare and best avoided. A better option is to use facilities at museums or the better cafés. If you do drop in specifically to use the toilet, it's customary to purchase coffee or some other drink before leaving.

Important note: you are always expected to put toilet tissue in the waste bin rather than down the toilet. Due to their narrow-bore pipes, toilets easily become clogged.

Where are the toilets?   **Pou íne i toualéttes?**

TOURIST INFORMATION

The national Visit Greece (www.visitgreece.gr; still sometimes known as the GNTO or EOT in Greek) has the following offices abroad:

Australia: 37–49 Pitt Street, Sydney, NSW 2000; tel: (02) 9241 1663.

Canada: 1500 Don Mills Road, Suite 102, Toronto, Ontario M3B 3K4; tel: (416) 968 2220.

UK: 4 Conduit Street, London W1R 0DJ; tel: 020 7495 9300.

US: 645 Fifth Avenue, New York, NY 10022; tel: (212) 421 5777.

These offices supply general information and glossy pictures, but when it comes to anything specific on Zákynthos or Kefaloniá they are usually of little help.

Zákynthos, strangely, does not have an official (EOT) tourism office, but you could try asking the tourist police for information. The Kefaloniá office in Argostóli (open daily 8am–2.30pm; on A. Trítsi, near the port authority; tel: 26710 22248) breaks the mould by being both helpful and informative. One recommended agency is Pama Travel in Fiskárdo, Kefaloniá (tel: 26740 41033, www.pamatravel.com).

TRANSPORT

Buses (*leoforía*). The public bus service on Zákynthos is patchy but, where it does exist, it is very good value. Timetables are displayed at bus stops (STASIS – *stásis*) and at the KTEL bus station in Zákynthos Town (tel: 26950 22255/42656), inconveniently located 2km up behind the centre. Most services run between Zákynthos Town and Laganás Bay and Vasilikós. For all buses, buy your tickets on board or from nearby kiosks. You can flag a bus down or disembark anywhere within reason.

The service on Kefaloniá is much better, making touring the island by public transport a real possibility. Direct buses run between Argostóli (on A. Trítsi, tel: 26710 22276) and all the other major towns (Póros, Sámi, Agía Efimía and Fiskárdo), and between Fiskárdo, Sámi, Póros and Skála. The Pallíki Peninsula is less well served but there is a service between Lixoúri and Xí. There is also a regular local service between Argostóli and Lássi. The fares are very reasonable and, generally, the service is frequent and punctual.

Taxis. These are an expensive way to get around but may be your only option in parts of Zákynthos. Make sure the meter is switched on; there are two rates depending on time of day and whether you are inside or outside town. Radio taxis can be summoned, for which there's a small surcharge.

Ferries. Regular ferries run between Pátra on the mainland and Sámi on Kefaloniá, and Kyllíni and Zákynthos Town. There are also services from Kyllíni to Póros on Kefaloniá and occasionally direct to Argostóli. There is also a ferry from Ágios Nikólaos (Skinári), in the north of Zákynthos, to the tiny port of Pesáda on Kefaloniá. A ferry runs between Sámi and Píso Aetós on Itháki. For current ferry schedules and fares check with your nearest travel agent, the port authority (see under Emergencies) or online at www.openseas.gr.

What's the fare to...?	Póso éhi éna isitírio giá...?
When's the next bus to...?	Póte févgi to epómeno leoforío giá...?

V

VISAS AND ENTRY REQUIREMENTS

All EU citizens can enter Greece to visit or work for an unlimited length of time. British citizens must be in possession of a valid passport. Citizens of Ireland can enter with a valid identity card or passport.

Citizens of the US, Canada, Australia and New Zealand can stay for up to three months on production of a valid passport. South African citizens can stay for up to two months on production of a valid passport. No visas are needed for these stays. If you wish to extend these timescales you must obtain a permit from the proper department of either Zákynthos Town or Argostóli police stations.

Greece has strict regulations about importing drugs. All the obvious ones are illegal, and there are strong punitive measures for anyone breaking the rules. Codeine and some tranquillisers are also banned. If you take any drug on the advice of your doctor, carry enough for your needs in an official container, as medicines for personal use are permitted.

Since the abolition of duty-free allowances for all EU countries, all goods brought into Greece from Britain and Ireland must be duty-paid. In theory there are no limitations to the amount of duty-paid goods that can be brought into the country. However, cigarettes and most spirits are much cheaper in Greece than in Britain and Ireland (government duty is much lower, so waiting until you reach your destination to buy these goods will save you money).

For citizens of non-EU countries, allowances for duty-free goods brought into Greece are: 200 cigarettes or 50 cigars or 250g of tobacco; 1 litre of spirits or 4 litres of wine; 250ml of cologne or 50ml of perfume.

Non-EU residents can claim back Value Added Tax (currently between 10 and 23 percent) on any items costing over €120, provided they export the item within 90 days of purchase. Tax-rebate forms are available at tourist shops and department stores. Keep the receipt and form. Make your claim at the customs area of the airport when departing.

Currency restrictions. There are no limits on the amount of euros visitors can import or export. There are no restrictions on travellers cheques, but cash sums of more than $10,000 or its equivalent should be declared on entry.

W

WEBSITES AND INTERNET ACCESS

Internet cafés. Internet access is now available in almost every beach resort. Charges are typically €2 to €4 per hour.

There are now a number of useful websites for people travelling to Zákynthos and Kefaloniá:

www.gnto.gr The official site of the EOT.

www.culture.gr The site of the Ministry of Culture, giving useful information on museums and archaeological sites.

www.openseas.gr An excellent site giving online timetables for most Greek ferry routes.

www.zanteweb.gr Pretty comprehensive site with a wealth of information on Zákynthos.

www.ithacagreece.com Excellent site giving all sorts of information, news and views of Itháki.

www.foi.org.uk The very useful site of Friends of the Ionian, an organisation that seeks to promote the islands' culture and identity, while protecting their environment.

Recommended Hotels

Although finding a room at short notice or on spec is not a problem for most of the summer, it is still wise to reserve well in advance for the peak season of the first three weeks in August. To telephone a hotel, dial the international country code for Greece (30), followed by the 10-digit number provided in our listings.

All hotels are classified by the Greek National Tourist Organization: luxury (L) class is at the very top, then A class down to E class (only hotels of L, A, B and C classes are featured below). In 2003, a star system (five-star equal to L, four-star to A, etc) was introduced but has been slow to catch on.

Rating establishes minimum price rates but prices can often vary widely within each class according to the season, location and availability of rooms. By law, rates must always be posted in all rooms; in practice this is often ignored.

The price categories below are for a double room with bath per night in high season. All hotel room rates include VAT (Value Added Tax) of 23 percent. All L- and A-class hotels have air conditioning. Most hotels in beach resorts are only open from April to October, and quite often even less than this. Those in Zákynthos Town and Argostóli are open all year round.

€€€€	above 130 euros
€€€	90–130 euros
€€	60–90 euros
€	below 60 euros

ZÁKYNTHOS

ZÁKYNTHOS TOWN

Hotel Alba €€ *Lámbrou Zivá 38, Zákynthos Town, tel: 26950 26641, www.albahotel.gr.* This small, newish B-class hotel is located in a fairly quiet area just two blocks in from the seafront. Facilities include air conditioning, television in the rooms and room service.

Hotel Palatino €€ *Kolokotróni 10 and Kolivá, Zákynthos Town, tel: 26950 27780, www.palatinohotel.gr.* A surprisingly good-value up-market place. The rooms, designed for business travellers, have all the trimmings, and the hotel as a whole is well tended and professionally run. A buffet breakfast is provided, and there is also a restaurant.

Hotel Plaza € *Kolokotróni 2, Zákynthos Town, tel: 26950 45733, www.plazazante.gr.* Probably the best value hotel in town, in the quiet Repáro district, a short distance in from the town beach. The compact rooms have air conditioning and TV.

Hotel Strada Marina €€ *Lombárdou 14, Zákynthos Town, tel: 26950 42761–3, www.stradamarina.gr.* The largest place in Zákynthos Town, with comfortable but not overly exciting rooms. In a vast modern building on the seafront, so many of the rooms have great views of the harbour. Breakfast is included, and there is a rooftop pool.

VASILIKÓS AND LAGANÁS BAY

Levantino Studio Apartments €€ *Kamínia beach, tel: 26950 35366, www.levantino.gr.* Ten quiet and attractive apartments close to the sea at the town end of the Vasilikós Peninsula. All are equipped with a kitchen, and some look out over the gardens and sea. Good discounts available out of high season.

Hotel Matilda €€ *Vasilikós district, tel: 26950 35376, www.matilda-hotel.gr.* A designer, B-class hotel on a hilltop, with commanding sea views from all its rooms and a large pool terrace.

Pansion Limni € *Límni Kerioú beach, tel: 26950 48716, www.pansion-limni.com.* Welcoming and superb value pension just behind the far end of the beach. There are some larger, newer apartments a little further inland. Guests often receive home-made olive oil and wine.

Porto Koukla Beach Hotel €€ *Lithakiá, tel: 26950 52393/51577, www.pavlos.gr.* This large hotel is situated at the western end of Laganás Bay. Popular mainly with German and Austrian visitors, Porto

Koukla is well away from the tawdriness further east. The hotel gardens back on to a narrow beach, which is overlooked by the hotel's excellent and cheap taverna.

Sirocco Hotel €€ *Kalamáki, tel: 26950 26083, www.siroccohotel.gr.* This is a good and reasonably quiet option in Kalamáki; the hotel's renovated and stylish standard rooms are a bargain out of season. There is a large swimming pool set in an attractive garden, and the beach is not too far away.

Villa Katerina € *Porto Roma, Vasilikós, tel: 26950 35456, www.villakaterina.com.* These two buildings, in pretty gardens, have simple rooms with kitchenettes and attached bathrooms. Set back from the beach the rooms are very quiet, and the surrounding area is lovely.

Vasilikos Beach €€ *Ágios Nikólaos, tel: 26950 35325, www.hotelvasilikosbeach.gr.* Large hotel with airy rooms that include all mod cons, a pool and a decent restaurant. The hotel also runs the popular water sports complex on the beach and arranges a free bus to bring people from Laganás and Kalamáki.

THE NORTH

Amoúdi Hotel € *Amoúdi, tel: 26950 62560, www.amoudihotel.com.* Tucked just inland from one of the nicer coves, between the busier resorts of Tsiliví and Alykés, this modern hotel offers spacious apartments, all with kitchenettes and balconies, and there is a fine pool.

Anenomilos (The Windmills) €€ *Korithí, Cape Skinári, tel: 26950 31132/31241, www.potamitisbros.gr.* One of the most attractive places to stay on Zákynthos. It consists of two converted windmills and some stone apartments at the very north end of the island. The friendly Potamitis family also run the excellent To Faros taverna and the cheapest trips to the nearby Blue Caves.

Anetis Beach Hotel € *Tsiliví, tel: 26950 28899, www.anetishotel.gr.* Compact but pleasant little place, set just back from the main beach in a lively but not noisy part of the resort. Many of the rooms have balconies facing the sea.

Louis Plagos Beach €€€€ *Aboúla Beach, Tsiliví, tel: 26950 62800, www.louishotels.com.* This is a large resort hotel with a huge range of facilities, particularly for children. The rooms are plain but large and have balconies, and there is the inevitable but good hotel pool and restaurant. Five day minimum stay.

Ionian Star Hotel € *Alykés, tel: 26950 83416/83658, www.ionian-star.gr.* A smallish and very well-kept hotel. The spotless rooms are excellent value (breakfast is included) and there is a restaurant which specialises in Greek food.

Nobelos Apartments €€€€ *Ágios Nikólaos (Skinári), tel: 26950 27632/31400, www.nobelos.gr.* These luxury apartments in the north of the island are hideously expensive but lovely. The four tastefully decorated suites are in a traditional stone-built house, each with an individual character. Along with excellent service, breakfast is provided and there's a secluded bay for swimming close by.

Panorama € *Ágios Nikólaos (Skinári), tel: 26950 31013, email: panorama-apts@ath.forthnet.gr.* A modest but friendly hotel in its own grounds on a bluff just south of the village with cosy rooms, many affording sea views. Great value with simple breakfast included.

Plessas Palace €€ *Alikanás, tel: 26950 29498, www.plessaspalace.com.* The spacious rooms are decorated in warm colours and other facilities include a pool, mini market and even a library. Near the village centre, almost a kilometre from the beach.

Zante Palace €€ *Tsiliví, tel: 26950 490490, www.zantepalace.com.* This huge modern hotel is on the bluff overlooking Tsiliví Bay, giving great views across to Kefaloniá. For what's on offer the rooms (which look out over the bay) are good value, and there is a nicely situated pool.

ARGOSTÓLI

Aenos Hotel €€ *Platía Vallianoú, Argostóli, tel: 26710 28013, www. aenos.com.* The uncluttered pastel-shaded rooms with large attached bathrooms probably give the Aenos the edge as the best place to stay on the town's central square; it is also marginally quieter. American buffet breakfast included.

Chara € *Corner of Dhevossétou and Y. Vergóti, Argostoli, tel: 26710 22427.* The last real budget option in town. Clean but extremely basic rooms with shared bathrooms. The amiable owner (who speaks little English) welcomes guests with a Greek coffee in the leafy courtyard.

Hotel Ionian Plaza €€ *Platía Vallianoú, Argostóli, tel: 26710 25581–4, www.ionianplaza.gr.* Excellent-value, C-class, designer hotel, with modern bathrooms and balconies overlooking the palm-studded square. The rooms are a bit on the small side, but the staff are friendly. Open all year.

Olga Hotel €€ *Andóni Trítsi 82, Argostóli, tel: 26710 24981–4, www. olgahotel.gr.* A medium-sized, functional seafront hotel, near to most of the action. The rooms are fairly standard but reasonable value and many have bay views.

LIXOÚRI AND THE SOUTH

Captain's House Hotel € *Skala, tel: 26710 83389, www.captain-shouse.net.* Captain's House Hotel is a friendly chocolate-coloured place with 28 rooms, located a couple of blocks from the resort's main street and not far from the beach. All are air-conditioned, with balconies and fridges.

Kastro Hotel €€ *Sámi, tel: 26740 22656/22282.* A little way out of town, but close to the sea, this is a medium-sized, good-value B-class hotel. The good, if smallish, rooms either look out over the pool and sea or the mountains. Breakfast is provided and there is also a restaurant.

La Cité €€ *Lixoúri, tel: 26740 92701, www.lacitehotellixouri.gr.* Four blocks uphill from the harbour, the good-value hotel has tastefully and colourfully furnished rooms and a uniquely shaped pool in its lush and exotic gardens.

Lara €€ *Lourdáta (Paralía Lourdás), tel: 26710 31157, www.lara.gr.* A peaceful, family-run C-class hotel, set in an olive grove some 300m (330yds) above the long sandy beach.

Mediterranée €€€€ *Lássi, tel: 26710 28760, www.mediterraneehotel. gr.* A vast hotel behind a small strip of beach. Facilities include a pool, tennis courts, two restaurants and shops. The rooms are high quality but greatly overpriced.

9 Muses €€€€ *Skála, tel: 26710 83563, www.9museshotel.com.* This is an attractively designed bungalow complex set in well-tended gardens just above mid-beach, with the room interiors doing justice to the surroundings. Officially C-class, but the 9 Muses is priced (and equipped) as B.

Odysseus Palace €€–€€€ *Póros, tel: 26740 72036, www.odysseuspalace.eu.* This modern hotel is the most comfortable place to stay in town. Good discounts may be available for the large and airy rooms (studios and apartments). Being away from the seafront, the hotel is quieter than most. Open all year.

Panas Hotel €€€ *Platía Spartiá, tel: 26710 69506/69448, www.panas-kefalonia.com.* A largish but pleasant B-class hotel on Lourdáta Bay, close to a good beach. The rooms, all of which have a balcony, are fine, if a little unimaginative. The hotel does, however, have good facilities for children, including their own pool and play area. There are also a couple of restaurants and a poolside bar.

Santa Irena € *Póros, tel: 26740 72017, email: maki@otenet.gr.* Cosy hotel offering compact but bright and comfortable rooms at unbeatable prices. Quiet inland location, a few blocks from the seafront. Only open in high season.

Hotel Summery €€ *Lixoúri, tel: 26710 91771/91871, www.hotel summery.gr.* A large but quiet hotel on Lixoúri's beach (to the south of town) that mainly caters to tour groups. The rooms are clean and unfussy, and some have balconies. For the amenities on offer (pool, plenty of sporty activities, and a shop) the prices are quite reasonable.

Tara Beach €€–€€€ *Skála, tel: 26710 83341/83250, www.tarabeach. gr.* A large but unobtrusive hotel right on the excellent beach. The rooms are decent, and, if you can't be bothered to waddle the few metres to the sea, there is a good pool in the pleasant gardens, beside which is a handy bar.

Trapezáki Bay Hotel €€€ *500m above Trapezáki beach, tel: 26710 31501–2, www.trapezakibayhotel.com.* Smart new upmarket resort with a full range of amenities, including pool, restaurant, bar and lavishly furnished rooms. The policy of maintaining one price all season makes it good value in high summer; airport transfer included.

THE NORTH

Agnantia Apartments €€€ *Tselendáta, Fiskárdo, tel: 26740 51802– 3, www.agnantia.com.* Very well maintained and beautifully located (although a little way out of Fiskárdo), these new hillside rooms are a lovely place to stay. As well as friendly and efficient service, the rooms are tasteful and comfortable, with a small kitchen area, and most have a balcony with wonderful views over to Itháki. A good, and generous, breakfast is included.

Athina Beach Hotel €€ *Karavómylos, tel: 26740 23067, www.athina hotel.gr.* Barely 2km (1.2 miles) from Sámi, close to a fine beach, this is the best place to stay on the bay. There is a small pool, the rooms are spacious and well-maintained and service is good. Sizeable discounts out of high season.

Cosi's Inn € *Ássos, tel: 26740 51430, www.cosisinn.gr.* One of the few places to stay in Ássos and certainly the best value. The simple rooms are set around a small courtyard, up the hill from the harbour.

Emelisse Art Hotel €€€€ *Éblissi, near Fiskárdo, tel: 26740 41200, www.arthotel.gr/emelisse.* Expensive (A-class) but chic, this boutique hotel is set in a traditional building. The well-designed rooms have luxurious bathrooms, and, inevitably, the infinity pool has a lovely view. For this sort of money you should expect to be pampered, and the service lives up to expectations.

Mina Studios € *Divaráta, tel: 26740 61716, markela1@hol.gr.* Just above the main junction in Divaráta, these spacious and well-furnished studios with kitchenettes are easily the best of the limited accommodation options close to stunning Mýrtos beach. Open Apr–Oct.

Moustakis Hotel €€ *Agía Efimía, tel: 26740 61060/61030, www.moustakishotel.com.* Smallish, and tucked away behind the harbourfront, this is the most pleasant hotel in town. All the rooms have air conditioning and balconies. Breakfast is available (extra charge). Discounts available for long stays.

Panormos € *Fiskárdo, tel: 26740 41203.* If you are looking for somewhere central, these six very reasonably priced rooms are above a restaurant right on Fiskárdo's picturesque waterfront – worth the price for the location alone.

Regina's € *Fiskárdo, tel: 26740 41125, www.regina-studios.gr.* Simple but comfortable rooms at the back of the village, near the village's attractive car park. There is a shady courtyard and the family that runs the place is very hospitable. The best deal in this upmarket resort.

To Archontiko €€€ *Fiskárdo, tel: 26740 41342, www.archontiko-fiskardo.gr.* Splendidly converted stone mansion backing onto the harbour. The rooms are stylishly decorated and air-conditioned, with sparkling bathrooms. There are a couple of rooms overlooking the harbour but noise comes with the view.

INDEX

Berlitz pocket guide

Zakynthos & Kefalonia

Third Edition 2013

Written by Maria Lord
Updated by Nick Edwards
Edited by Alexia Georgiou
Picture Researcher: Lucy Johnston
Series Editor: Tom Stainer
Production: Tynan Dean, Linton Donaldson
and Rebeka Ellam

Photography credits: Gkordus/Dreamstime.
com 21; buso23/Bigstockphoto 5TC; Danita
Delimont/Alamy 37; Dimitris K./Alamy
35; Elina Manninen/Bigstockphoto 4-5T;
emberiza/Fotolia 7TC, 97; GNTO 2TC, 94; Jan
Wlodarczyk/Alamy 43; iStockphoto 8, 26, 39,
48, 58, 80, 82, 89, 93, 98; Kevin Cummins/Apa
Publications 1, 2TL, 2/3T, 3TC, 2/3M, 4ML, 4MR,
4TL, 5MC, 6ML, 10, 13, 14, 16, 19, 24, 50, 54,
56, 62, 64, 67, 69, 71, 72, 75, 76, 78, 79, 84, 87,
90, 91, 100, 101; mce128/Bigstockphoto 6ML,
11; Mike Kiev/Bigstockphoto 36; Mockford &
Bonnetti/Apa Publications 2MC, 2ML, 3M, 22,
23, 30, 33, 41, 44, 59, 60, 61, 65, 83; netfalls/
Bigstockphoto 29; Sylvaine Poitau 4/5M, 102;
Tony Lilley/Alamy 46; Chris Cheadle/Alamy 3M

Cover picture: 4Corners Images

Contact us

At Berlitz we strive to keep our guides as
accurate and up to date as possible, but if you
find anything that has changed, or if you have
any suggestions on ways to improve this guide,
then we would be delighted to hear from you.

Berlitz Publishing, PO Box 7910,
London SE1 1WE, England.
email: berlitz@apaguide.co.uk
www.insightguides.com/berlitz